how to Honey Boo Boo™

how to Honey Boo Boo™

The Complete Guide on How to REDNECKOGNIZE the Honey Boo Boo in You

The Shannon & Thompson Family
with Jennifer Levesque

From the hit TLC™ series **here comes Honey Boo Boo**

WILLIAM MORROW

An Imprint of HarperCollinsPublishers

HarperCollins books may be purchased for educational, business, or sales promotional use. For information please write: Special Markets Department, HarperCollins Publishers, 10 East 53rd Street, New York, NY 10022.

FIRST EDITION

Designed by Lorie Pagnozzi

Library of Congress Cataloging-in-Publication Data has been applied for.

ISBN 978-0-06-228850-9

13 14 15 16 17   OV/RRD   10 9 8 7 6 5 4 3 2 1

Warning! Mud boggin', inner tubing, and all the fun and games talked about in this book are performed by professional rednecks in a controlled redneck environment. These activities may be dangerous or may be inappropriate for young children. All of these activities should be carried out under adult supervision only. The material contained in this book is presented for entertainment purposes and the authors and publishers expressly disclaim liability, loss or risk, personal or otherwise, incurred as a consequence, directly or indirectly, from engaging in the activities contained in this book. In other words, don't come crying to us if your kid has two thumbs, or if a pet teacup pig ruins your couch, or if you overdose on sketti.

Dedicated to all our beautimous fans.
We redneckognize you!

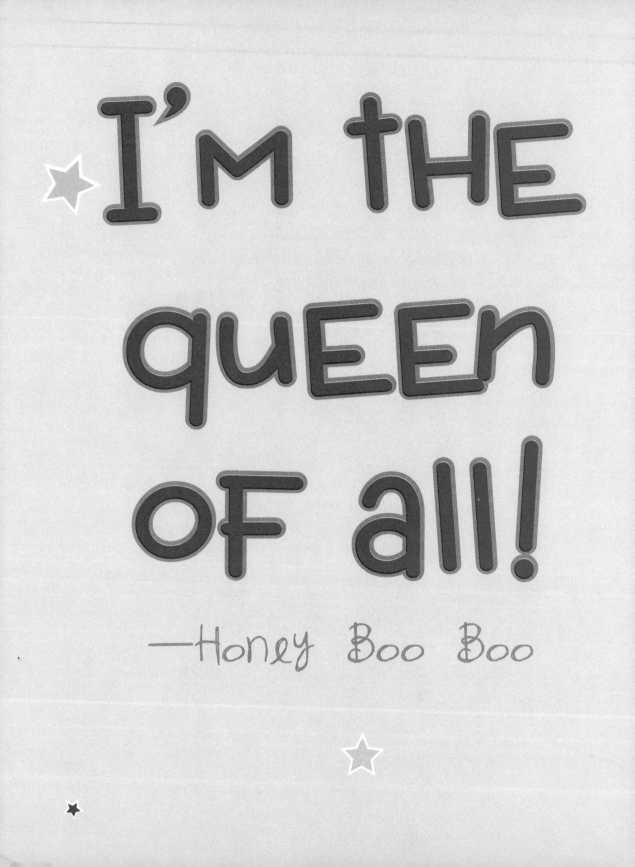

Contents

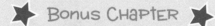

FAMILY

Mike "Sugar Bear" Thompson

Born on December 13, 1971, Mike is from Georgia, works at a chalk mine, and is June's baby daddy for Alana.

LIKES: June, being a dad, dipping tobacco, riding four-wheelers, volunteering as a firefighter, dressing up as Santa at charity events, deer statues, June's voluptuous curves, wrestling matches, The Dukes of Hazzard, jelly beans.

DISLIKES: not having enough alone time with June, getting hit in the face with pumpkin goo, hot weather.

Jessica "Chubbs" Shannon

Older sister of Alana and second daughter of June. Described by June as the most responsible of her daughters, she's involved in ROTC and wants to be a nurse when she grows up. She's Alana's BFF.

LIKES: eating, fashion design, hair bows, hanging out with Alana.

DISLIKES: frogs, collard greens, dieting, parallel parking, being called Chubbs.

Nugget the Chicken

New family pet.

LIKES: walking around, clucking, pecking food out of the carpet in the living room, laying golden eggs.

DISLIKES: being used as a tree topper, being potty trained, watching the family eat chicken.

Alana "Honey Boo Boo" Thompson

Mama June's youngest child and Sugar Bear's only child. Definitely the most sassified of all the girls. Girl Scout, pageant queen, elementary school attendee. You betta redneckognize!

LIKES: pets, dancing, cheese balls, making faces in the mirror, swimming, playing in the mud, speaking "Spanish," talking with her belly.

DISLIKES: etiquette lessons, salad and vegetables, gnats, hot weather, anything boring.

June "Mama" Shannon

Born on August 10, 1979, she's a mother of four (and grandmother of one) and the matriarch of this family. Sugar Bear's her squeeze of nearly ten years and June's baby daddy for Alana.

LIKES: being a mom, sneezing, giving back to the community, all forms of thriftiness, bingo, tracking down roadkill.

DISLIKES: mayonnaise, hot weather, wasted toilet paper, oranges, spending money when she can get things for free, the "M" word.

Anna "Chickadee" Shannon

Older sister of Alana and June's eldest daughter. Mother of baby Kaitlyn. An expert at Guess Whose Breath?, she is attempting to be the first in her family to graduate from high school.

LIKES: being a mom, boys, being lazy, wrestling.

DISLIKES: doing chores, being creative, giving birth, Glitzy, trains.

Lauryn "Pumpkin" Shannon

Older sister of Alana and June's third daughter. Origin of her nickname is her favorite and recurring Halloween costume.

LIKES: cranberry sauce, sketti, farting, general mayhem.

DISLIKES: lightning, behaving etiquettely.

Baby Kaitlyn Elizabeth

Daughter of Anna and first granddaughter of Mama June and Sugar Bear. She shares the same middle name as June and got her ears pierced the same day as Alana. She has been in one pageant already.

LIKES: playing, laughing, crying, pooping, sucking her thumbs, high sixes.

DISLIKES: spitting up, gloves.

y the Pig

y pet (at least for a

A-LA-NA!!, ooo-ing les, food, squealing, nail polish,

KES: being quiet, being n away, being made into on.

FOREWORD

Hi, y'all! I'm so happy to be writing the foreword to *How to Honey Boo Boo*! This is the ultimate collection of everything you need to know to live like we do, from our games to our recipes to our philosophy. Like us, this book is a lot of fun and doesn't take itself too seriously!

I've heard from fans all over the country about how much they love Alana and *Here Comes Honey Boo Boo*. The outpouring of support makes us so happy, and we're glad we're able to entertain people. One thing folks always ask me is, how close is this to real life? Is this how you guys actually *are*? Well, I can tell you that what you see is definitely what you get. We are a very close family, we like to get muddy, and we act exactly in real life as we do on the show. All my kids have their own personalities, and I allow them to be who they are, whether on or off camera.

Our family also believes strongly in giving back to our community. This is another big priority for us. We were in need once and someone helped us out, so now we try to be there for others who are in that situation. And who knows, that could be us again one day—you never know what life is going to bring. I hope that reading about some of our community work inspires you to get involved, reach out to others, and help your own community.

While the show is important to me and I love it, my kids are always my number one priority. My advice to anybody is, whatever you do, make your kids number one over anybody else. You can never go wrong with this advice. Life is about making memories and having fun with your family. So I hope you have fun reading the book, I hope you make some sketti, and I hope this gives you some ideas to make some fun memories with your own family.

—June "Mama" Shannon

INTRODUCTION

A dolla make me holla,
Honey Boo Boo child!

—Alana, a.k.a. Honey Boo Boo

Welcome to *How to Honey Boo Boo*, the ultimate guide to America's loudest, gassiest, funniest, most loving, and most generous redneck family. When Alana, Mama June, and Sugar Bear burst onto the scene, most people were instantly drawn to the outrageous and oversize personality of pint-size pageant queen Alana Thompson, a.k.a. Honey Boo Boo. America just couldn't believe what was coming out of her mouth. But it all made sense once they got to know the rest of her family: beautimous coupon queen Mama June, mud boggin' Sugar Bear, frog-fearing Jessica, most pregnantest Anna, and lightning-struck Pumpkin.

When *Here Comes Honey Boo Boo* premiered in 2012, everyone—critics and viewers alike—had a definite opinion about the family. Not that the Shannon/Thompson family cares. Some have found *Here Comes Honey Boo Boo* to be horrifying, while others can appreciate just how much love and warmth are present in the Honey Boo Boo household. So, what's their life philosophy? Have fun with the time you have and spend it with your family. Teach your kids the correct values: how to be feugel, how to just be yourself, how to have fun, the importance of family, and, most important, never to buy used panties at a flea market.

Hope you enjoyed our handy Shannon/Thompson family tree. (Just don't tell Nugget that she's on the bottom.) Now that you have the family members straight, do you want to learn what it takes to live your life the Honey Boo Boo way? Hells yeah you do! In these pages, we've crammed in everything you need to know to be an official unofficial member of the Honey Boo Boo family. Want to learn to make the perfect sketti? Turn to page 48. How about finding out what your redneck name would be? Well, page 16 is the place for you. Or would you rather get tips on mud boggin', taking care of a teacup pig, or setting up your own lemonade stand? It's all here, slathered in butter, in one easy-to-use guide. You'll find out how to end up with a fatter wallet after a visit to the grocery store, what to do with your kids when they're crazy bored, and which redneckulously delicious recipes to cook for your own family. We're also going to explore the over-the-top things the family has done on the show, as well as give you a detailed analysis of Pumpkin's best sayings ("The Ten Greatest Quotes of Miss Lauryn Shannon"). You will be so up on this family that you'll be farting and burping all the way to the Redneck Games in no time. You betta redneckognize!

Chapter 1

TALK LIKE HONEY BOO BOO

A lot of our fans out there asked the reason why we are subtitled so much, 'cause they can't understand a single word. But I think, just like anybody, like the northerners and the Californians, some people can't understand the Southern drawl.

—Mama June

I understand everything June says.

—Sugar Bear

One of the things that has endeared the Shannon/Thompson clan to so many people across the country is the quirky, crazy, and redneckulous way the family speaks every single day. No, not just *loudly*—though Mama June admits, if you're not hollerin' they ain't listenin'. Hang around the family and you'll notice that they have their own unique way of speaking. For anyone who wants to learn how to sound like a true member of this clan—or just understand what *too-tay* means—we present a super-detailed dictionary of Shannon/Thompson speak that explains how to talk Honey Boo Boo–style. You might be *apprehensum* about learning to talk like Alana and friends, but don't worry at all—you will be *beautimous* and *smexy* in no time. Once you learn to understand their regional patois (subtitles will only get you so far), you might even be able to interpret their lingo for your friends. Each word

1

or phrase is followed by a brief definition and then a summary of how (and why) that word or phrase was used on the show. It's the redneckopedia we've all been waiting for!

The Ultimate Redneckopedia

Apocalypse

1) The end of the world, which the Mayans predicted would happen in 2012. 2) When the zombies attack. When the apocalypse does come, Mama June's stockpiled toilet paper rolls will be in high demand, and she plans to sell them for five hundred dollars apiece. The girls tease Mama June about the rows and rows (and rows) of toilet paper she keeps in the pantry, all bought on the cheap using extreme couponing (see chapter 4). But June points out that the girls will be more than happy to have these items when the apocalypse hits, since people will pay big money for staples. The apocalypse is comin' soon, so be prepared!

Apprehensum

The redneck way of saying *apprehensive*. See also *obstamistical*. Mama June coins this term when talking about Alana's first trip to an ice-skating rink. Alana was a bit . . . *apprehensum* about it. Mama June says, "Alana was pretty skeptical the first time, but once she got onto the ice, I couldn't get her off." Indeed, Alana has the time of her life and looks like a li'l pageant princess out on the ice. Don't be apprehensum next time somebody tries to get you into ice skates. It's like learning to ride a bike, except you'll fall down a lot and the ice is really cold.

Armpit Serenade

When one puts one's fist under one's arm and squeezes, with the objective of making a farting sound. It's unknown why any member of the Shannon/Thompson clan would need to fake a farting sound.

Arshal-Ficial Inseminator

A tool that can be used to help women get pregnant, but you can also use it to baste your turkey. June can't find one, so she has to baste her turkey using a regular spoon: "Oh, you're looking good. You got butter in your ass. I gotta come up with an invention because I can't find no arshal-ficial inseminator today."

Bamm-Bamm look

To be out in a public place with no shoes or socks on to speak of, à la Bamm-Bamm Flintstone. This term was coined by the manager of the family's local gas station/convenience store. On some hot days (or just to pass the time), Mama June lets the girls walk down the road to the store to shop, chitchat with the clerks, and walk up and down the aisles. Pumpkin always goes in completely barefoot, without a care in the world. As one of the clerks said, "Pumpkin is my country girl. It feels better barefoot! We're in the country, that's how we do it." No shirt, no shoes, no problem, indeed.

Barn

The human body. Mama June often says she's going to "put a little paint on this old barn," meaning she's going to get dressed up or put makeup on or somehow put a little extra effort into her appearance. When Alana goes to get a facial in preparation for an upcoming pageant, she says, "They gotta shine up this old barn for the judges."

Beautimous

A combination of *beautiful* and *fabulous*. As Mama June says, "Granted, I ain't the most beautimous out of the box, but a little paint on this barn [see above], shine it back to its original condition. 'Cause it shines up like it's brand new." And when Mama and the girls go to a water park and notice all of the bigger women who are scantily clad, June says, "All that vajiggle-jaggle [see page 13] is not . . . beautimous."

Bingo Face

Intense squinting to see the bingo board that creates a look of fierce determination. When Mama June is playing bingo—her favorite sport in the world, aside from extreme couponing—she takes it very seriously and squints so she's sure to see each number that's being called. Mama June is legally blind, so she squints at almost everything of import—bowling scores, pageant stages, you name it. But bingo is definitely one of Mama's big talents. As Pumpkin says, "Mama plays bingo better than she cooks or cleans or *anything*."

Biscuit

That special part of a woman's anatomy. See also *moon pie, pa-doose, too-tay, va-jay-jay*.

When the family takes a pregnant Anna to get an ultrasound, Alana sees the baby's image on the screen and says, "Where's her biscuit?" Why is it called a biscuit? Well, it looks like a biscuit! As Mama June somewhat cryptically explains, "You look at a biscuit, and if it's cooked right, like [at a fast-food restaurant] or something . . . it opens up." Later on, when baby Kaitlyn is finally born, Alana exclaims, "Baby Kaitlyn arrived on the biscuit express!"

Chef Boy Bar Dean

Off-brand ravioli. Mama June claims that off-brands are sometimes better than the name brands and offer a great value. Pumpkin disagrees and says that Chef Boy Bar Dean is subpar. She says, "No, they're freaking gross." Note: please don't confuse Chef Boy Bar Dean with their competitor Chef For Ar Dee.

Cup-A-Fart™

Weaponized farting; when one catches a fart in his or her hands and then throws it at the enemy's face. Mama June calls it "biological warfare at its best." When meeting some wrestlers backstage at a local event, Alana suggests using this move to knock out opponents. However, in a surprise attack, Sugar Bear unleashes a "monster Cup-A-Fart™" that forces both the family and the wrestlers to clear the room. As Mama June says, "We're gonna revolutionize the wrestling world with the Cup-A-Fart™. You just wait and see. Wrestlers will be passing out everywhere."

Cycle of Life

The natural progression of animals through nature. The old make way for the young. Big animals eat smaller animals. Big animals get hit by cars and eaten by people. As Mama June says: "We bring it home, skin it, cook it, eat it, save money; that's the way the cycle of life works in our family."

Dip

Chewing tobacco. Whenever it looks like Sugar Bear has something in his mouth, it's probably dip. It's gross. Sugar Bear would probably get more smooches if he replaced the dip with a quality bubble gum (see *Hubba Bubba* on page 7).

Doo-doo girl

An individual who smells like dog poop because she stepped in it. Also, a term of endearment applied to the one who has stepped in it. Mama June calls Pumpkin doo-doo girl when she steps in a big pile of dog poo right before heading to one of Alana's pageants. "She smelled like a poop party!" Alana wryly observes.

Door nut

We still have no idea what this means. When Alana is being interviewed on camera for the show, she says, "I'm talking in Spanish. Oh my door nuts!" When the producer asks, "What is a door nut, Alana?" she teases him, repeating, "What is a door nut, Alana? Like, totally, OMG." It's enough to make you go totally door nuts.

Dukesy Hazzard

Sugar Bear's favorite television show, as pronounced by Alana. His favorite character is Daisy Duke because, as Mama June says, "he actually got to meet her one time in person,

and swear to God, he almost ******** on himself." For Shugie's forty-first birthday the family decides to throw him a *Dukes of Hazzard*–themed party, complete with a custom piñata shaped as Daisy Duke's iconic short-shorts. You're never too old for a piñata. As Sugar Bear says, "I just closed my eyes, imagined Daisy Duke, and started whackin' it."

Elvis

1) A popular singer from the 1950s to 1970s. 2) Santa Claus's helper! When Alana is practicing her brand-new routine for the Rock Star Divas and Dolls Pageant, her new dance coach asks her if she knows who Elvis is. Alana says, "Elvis is Santa's helper!" And then she adds, "I know this because my daddy told me." Later on, when one of the show's producers asks Alana how Elvis makes toys for the children, she thinks for a moment and says, "I do not know. I don't go to the North Pole." We think she will in season 4.

Etiquettely

Having good manners. In an early *Here Comes Honey Boo Boo* episode, Mama June invites an etiquette instructor over to the house to teach Alana and Pumpkin some manners. (Although Pumpkin is pretty sure she doesn't need classes 'cause "what you see is what you get." The instructor replies, "Well, I hope that works for you.") The instructor tells them that etiquette is about kindness and respect, and tries to teach them a few lessons about manners when meeting people and also when dining. As June points out, the etiquette instructor is a little more of a "square" than the Shannon/Thompson clan, who are a bit more *wopsided*—"lopsided, obtuse, triangle, oval all put together." And absolutely nobody can be proper and "etiquettely" all the time.

Eww

To poop. See also *ooo*. While they're awaiting the birth of Anna's baby, Mama June explains to the girls that a woman will sometimes eww on herself as she's giving birth to a baby. This is, of course, before her hemorrhoids come out. Needless to say, the girls are thoroughly grossed out, and Pumpkin begs Mama to "shut up!"

Fart ghost

A ghost that you can actually smell before it scares you. Even more horrifyingly, Alana claims fart ghost also farts out certain condiments. "Fart ghost is here!" says Alana. "And he just farted mayonnaise!" Hmm, this fart ghost seems to follow the family around everywhere . . .

Fat cake

Processed and packaged cake you purchase at the grocery or convenience store. Mama June and family stock up on fat cakes of all kinds when they take part in the local food auctions (see page 73). Soon after, Mama June and the girls put themselves on a diet, but June catches Pumpkin eating one of these delicious prepackaged treats: "What the hell you eating that fat cake for?" And Alana adds, "You're on a diet. Give me that fat cake!" Pumpkin also says that on her thirteenth birthday, she wants to go to the fat cake factory.

Feugel

Being thrifty and careful with your money. When the family visits a flea market around Christmastime, Mama June gives each of her daughters ten dollars to spend but tells them to try to spend only five. She does this to teach them the value of a dollar and how to be *feugel* with their money. A very important skill for any good li'l redneck to have!

Flesh-eating disease

Horrible bacteria that will eat your skin if you're infected with them. When Mama June takes the family to the Redneck Games in East Dublin, Georgia, it's a blazing hot day, and by the end, the girls want to go swimming in a nearby body of water. Mama June forbids it, saying she heard there is a flesh-eating bacteria in the water. June really looks out for her family and just doesn't want them to take the risk of contracting a horrible disease. The older girls are willing to risk it. As they walk away from the water, Alana yells out to the remaining swimmers, "I hope y'all get that flesh-eating disease! I'll laugh!" Yelling this out was not very etiquettely.

Forklift foot

A condition that occurs when one's toe is run over by a forklift and never properly treated. "C'mon, Mama, show us your forklift foot!" says Alana. Years ago when Mama June worked in a warehouse, her foot was accidentally run over by a forklift. It hurt badly and June's foot never fully recovered from it. Now Mama June never takes her socks off and even wears them while swimming. Needless to say, Pumpkin, Jessica, and Honey Boo Boo are obsessed with seeing this mangled foot, but June is self-conscious about it and won't take her socks off for any reason—even for a pedicure or in 103-degree heat. (See also "Mani-Pedis June-Style" on page 94.) Finally, on a visit to a water park, Mama June relents and takes the sock off. The girls have *never* seen Mama's foot before this moment, and the family is completely grossed out when they see the toe in all its glory. Her big toe is mangled and there are several gnats swarming around it—yuck! Pumpkin quickly sums up the situation by saying, "If I had a toe like that, I'd chop it off." Forklift foot also keeps Mama from ever wearing heels—she's much more comfortable in a pair of bedazzled Keds.

Frisky McBrisky

How babies are made. "We don't do that kind of business in our house," says Mama June.

Funeral Shirt

Even more serious than the professional shirt. Only to be worn on very special occasions. Alana says, "When Shugie wears his funeral shirt, you know he's serious." Sugar Bear wears his funeral shirt to impress June, and the girls approve. "You look good, you look like a robin's egg," says Jessica. Mama June is a little suspicious when she sees it. "What you got your funeral shirt on for?" she says. "Special occasion," answers Sugar Bear.

Gigi

The family's redneck word for *grandma*. Baby Kaitlyn sneezes just like Mama June, prompting her to say, "Do it like Gigi does it, that's right!"

Grass Fight

Summer version of a snowball fight, mud fight, or food fight. When Uncle Poodle comes to teach Alana a new dance routine for her pageant, Pumpkin starts making fun of him for brushing leaves off his shirt. So he takes a huge clump of grass and throws it right at her. Of course, she throws some back at him ("Not this shirt!" he yells), and soon, Pumpkin, Poodle, and Alana are in the midst of a huge grass fight. As Uncle Poodle tells it, Alana thinks she won the fight since she's a princess, but he thinks he actually won. Perhaps it was a tie. When having your own grass fight, please be careful not to throw rocks, which are worse than keys. And don't ruin anyone's professional shirt.

High Six

A high five with an extra thumb. Jessica invents a special high five for baby Kaitlyn, who has an extra thumb on her right hand. High sixes all around!

Hook 'Em and Book 'Em

Mama June's phrase for a one-night stand, which is what Sugar Bear was supposed to be. "I've been with Sugar Bear almost nine years now," Mama June says. "It was just supposed to be like a random hookup thing. Here we go nine years later and a kid."

Horny Bear

Sugar Bear's alter ego. "When June came out as Marilyn Monroe, I instantly became Horny Bear," says Sugar Bear. Va va voom!

Hot Mess

Something that is completely out of sorts and just not right. Mama June uses this phrase several times when discussing any number of topics, from the never-before-pedicured feet of her daughters, to some of the crazy wigs that are available at Shh! It's a Wig, to the scarecrow that is built in her honor.

Hubba Bubba

1) A popular brand of bubble gum. 2) A redneck variation on *hubba hubba*, yelled out when someone is especially beautimous. As Sugar Bear says when he sees June with her new blond hairdo: "Hubba Bubba! That's a sexy mama now." Horny Bear elaborates: "June looked like a blond bombshell. Va va voom. You better chain me to a bed because I'm coming up . . . I'm in attack mode tonight." Mama June's response? "Ah, pssshhhht." Sugar Bear also says this when he sees the piñata that's been made for his forty-first birthday party: "That's Daisy Duke . . . Hubba Bubba!"

Ideal

Redneck way of saying *idea*. As in: "Alana was dying to see a live turkey, so I had the harebrained ideal to get up at the ass-crack of dawn and take her to the farm on one of our off days. The worst ideal ever." (Jessica points out, "We could have slept!") Mama also uses this word when discussing Sugar Bear's *Dukes of Hazzard*–themed birthday party: "That's normally how we do it, um, we start with an ideal and we just work it with whatever we got around the house."

"It is what it is"

June's philosophy of life. Related to: "*que será será*," "*c'est la vie*," "I yam what I yam." June's most important phrase, used to encom-

pass the totality of life and the acceptance of one's place within the grand scheme of things. She says this many times during the course of *Here Comes Honey Boo Boo*, and it means that things happen in life and one has to accept them and move on.

Junecrow

A scarecrow built in the likeness of Mama June. One day, Uncle Poodle helps the girls make scarecrows to put on the lawn for fall. Alana wants to make one that looks like June, so she goes into Mama's drawer and steals some of her clothes, including a bra! They even put a blond wig on it. With the scarecrow almost complete, they paint the Junecrow's toes over her socks to hide the forklift foot . . . just like Mama. As Alana says, "Building a scarecrow was easy peasy," but Mama isn't too pleased. "That's not me," she says. "Yeah, it is," answers Jessica. If only a Junecrow could scare trains away.

Kitchen sink

1) A sink in a kitchen for washing dishes, vegetables, etc. 2) A place for washing one's hair. With five girls and only one bathroom, it's simply not possible for everyone to take a bath or shower every single day. So the clan has to get creative with cleanliness. "Our hair has always been washed in the kitchen sink," Mama June says. "It's not like dirtiness or nothing. When you take a bath, you're sitting in your own filth so you don't want your hair to be nasty."

Kribbit's Rot

Where the Indians and Pilgrims ate their first Thanksgiving dinner, according to Alana.

Alana has to do a school project on Thanksgiving, so Mama June gives her and her sister a little quiz about the first Turkey Day, which they both manage to completely bomb. (See "Take June's Thanksgiving Quiz" on page 36.)

Marannaise

Mayonnaise. It's just like ketchup, but it's white. June's kryptonite. Alana eats it straight and claims it tastes like vanilla ice cream.

Moon Pie

That special part of a woman's anatomy. See also *biscuit, pa-doose, too-tay, va-jay-jay*. Alana is very excited when Anna is about to give birth and hollers, "Kaitlyn's comin' out of Anna's moon pie any day now!" One of the many creative and memorable words the family has for this body part.

Mootie Moot

A pet name for Alana. See also *Smoochie*. Although *Smoochie* is the preferred term of endearment during pageants, Mama June sometimes likes to yell out a good "Hey, Mootie Moot!" to Alana when she's onstage. Alana, for her part, will answer to either Smoochie or Mootie Moot—or not, depending on how she's feeling.

Mud boggin'

Driving a vehicle through a mud hole. Also known as mud racing or mud running. Sugar Bear loves this activity. The entire family gets on four-wheelers (sometimes in combinations of two or three people) and drives through mud pits. Often they end up getting into great big mud fights, or they attach inner tubes to the backs of the vehicles for a real fun ride. The family calls mud boggin' a "redneck baptism," because you ain't a real redneck until you've gotten muddy. As Alana says, "I like to get dirty like a pig!"

Multi-Meal

A meal that's prepared, baked, and served all in one dish. "It's a multi-meal," Mama June says. "I'm not sure how other families do it. I mean, ya know, I just put everything in a bowl and I don't have to worry about putting the sides all over the plate. You just put them all in together." (See "Multi-Meals" and other recipes in chapter 3.)

Neck Crust

A dark crust that forms in the folds of one's neck fat. Pumpkin admits she has no idea where Mama June's neck crust comes from (does she not scrub her neck while taking a bath?), but she helpfully suggests purchasing some rust remover at the grocery store to get rid of it. Mama June's succinct reply to Pumpkin? "You're stupid."

Obstamistical

Redneck way of saying *skeptical*. When Alana is about to go ice-skating for the first time, she is all kinds of nervous. As Mama June says, "Alana was pretty skeptical the first time, but once she got onto the ice, I couldn't get her off." When Jessica asks, "What's apstamentical?" June tries to explain: "Obstamistical . . . like . . . you don't want to do it at first and then you end up doin' it."

Old man glue

Denture cream, used to hold a flipper (fake teeth) in place for pageants. Put old man glue on the flipper, stick it in your mouth, smile, and presto! You're all ready for a pageant. As Alana says, "Old man glue makes me feel funny"—which means that it makes her run around in a circle in her living room until she's dizzy. Sounds like old man glue is more potent than Honey Boo Boo Lemonade (see page 49).

Ooo

1) To poop. 2) When a pet teacup pig poops on your kitchen table. See also *eww*. Alana puts her li'l bundle of joy, Glitzy the pig, on the table as the family is sitting around it. Everyone is laughing and talking happily when suddenly— eeeeeeew! "We put Glitzy on the table and she ooo'd herself," says Alana. The girls can't agree on whether Glitzy's ooo looks like a burnt hot dog or a chocolate éclair, but one thing is for certain: Alana will never eat in that spot again! This is one of several incidents that dooms Glitzy and determines his ultimate fate.

Pa-doose

That special part of a woman's anatomy. See also *biscuit, moon pie, too-tay, va-jay-jay*. When discussing the birth of Alana with Mama and Sugar Bear, Pumpkin says, "[She] came out of your pa-doose, it didn't come out of his!"

Pigzilla

A four-pound sandwich, served at Papa Buck's BBQ in Georgia. Pigzilla is comprised of three pounds of pulled pork on a one-pound bun. In order to win $200, you have to eat everything on the plate in forty-five minutes and then keep it down for five minutes (before you can throw up). As of this writing, only one person has defeated Pigzilla, and that person was a professional eater. It's Pumpkin's dream to be the first woman to eat Pigzilla and, as always, Mama June supports her: "You could be the redneck Kobayashi if you freakin' listen to me." Pumpkin finally gets her wish on her birthday when her family takes her to Papa Buck's. As Mama says, "She kind of like paves the way for the other women that have been always wanting to eat Pigzilla but hadn't done it, so maybe the other women will step up and try the Pigzilla too."

Poodle

A homosexual man. Sugar Bear's younger brother is gay, and since *poodle* is Alana's slang term for "homosexual," Alana started calling him "Uncle Poodle." As Alana tells it, "My gay uncle is Poodle. That's why we call him a poodle, because he has a little fruit in his tank. He's got grapes in his tank." Uncle Poodle loves Alana and participates in many family activities, including trying to teach Alana a new dance routine. But is a poodle the only type of gay pet you can have? As Jessica says, "There might be other gay dogs . . . like shih tzus . . . and koala bears."

Professional shirt

A shirt that means business. See also *funeral shirt*. Pumpkin wears one when pursuing her dream of eating Pigzilla. "Are you ready for today?" Mama June asks Pumpkin. "You gonna do it? You better put your professional shirt on and do what you gotta do." When someone wears their professional shirt, you know they're serious. Professional shirts should be unwrinkled with a professional iron.

Pssshhhht

June's favorite noise; has a dismissive connotation. Used to express disbelief, such as when Sugar Bear tries to be romantic with June. When Sugar Bear brings home a Thanksgiving turkey that's frozen, Mama June says, "Pssshhhht, there's gonna be a burnt bird on my table."

Rebelchious

The state of being in rebellion. Uncle Poodle uses this dubious term when discussing the big grass fight he got into with Alana and Pumpkin. As he tells it, "Being the rebelchious uncle that I am, I filled Pumpkin's ass with grass!"

Redneck air conditioner

A wet towel wrapped around one's head. On a particularly hot day, Mama June walks around the beach with a wet towel wrapped around her head. Says Mama, "It keeps you cool, it keeps you wet, wet T-shirt contest all in one." This is one of many redneck quick fixes that are featured on *Here Comes Honey Boo Boo*.

Redneck bathtub

Any body of water on public property that a lot of people share. When the kids want to go swimming at the Redneck Games, Mama forbids it, saying, "I would prefer my kids not to be in the redneck bathtub." Probably because of the flesh-eating bacteria.

Redneckognize

To respectfully acknowledge something to be of redneck origin. When talking about playing in the mud as a family and riding around on four-wheelers, Alana exclaims, "I like to get down and dirty, redneck-style . . . you betta redneckognize!" This has become a hallmark of the show and one of its most popular catchphrases.

Roadkill

Alana describes roadkill as "any animal that didn't look both ways before crossing the road." Part of the road-to-table movement. See also *cycle of life* on p. 3. The Shannon/Thompson family frequently incorporates roadkill into their meal plan, usually deer or hog, but Alana has big ideas: "My roadkill wish list is . . . a rabbit, a hamster, a monkey—they go crazy. A bird; a butterfly; uh, a porcupine, 'cause you can pick your teeth with the quills; and a wild pig; raccoon; a gopher; a elephant; a lion. This is making me hungry too."

Sassified

When one wears clothes that make one feel (and look) extra sassy. When Alana gets too big to fit into her glitz pageant dress, she and her mama go out to buy a new one from Miss Lacey at her small boutique. First Alana tries on the shell of the dress, which is hot pink—but the jewels are on hand to be sewn on later and make the dress look extra glamorous. Alana looks great in the dress (as June says, "I know it will be beautimous when we get it, because Lacey's dresses are the bomb-diggity"), and Miss Lacey pins Alana all over so the dress will fit perfectly. Unfortunately, she also pokes Alana several times with the pins and Alana threatens to poke Lacey back. "Don't be sassy," Miss Lacey tells Alana, but it's too late—as Alana says, "I'm *sassified*!"

Sausage Sized

The size of June's ring finger. When the family goes bowling, June's fingers won't fit in the smaller ball because she has, as Alana says, "sausage hands." Sausage hands sometimes lead to sausage fingers, and when a store clerk asks Alana what size ring Mama June might like, Alana proudly replies, "Sausage sized!"

Shack-'em-up Mates

Two people who cohabitate without being legally defined spouses. "Sugar Bear is my baby's daddy and we've been shack-'em-up mates for, like, eight years now," says Mama June.

SHH! It's a Wig

A wig shop in Georgia. This is the wig store that Mama June takes Alana to so she can find a new hairpiece for her next pageant. While they don't end up finding anything that would be suitable for Alana, they do try on a lot of wigs and have a great time. Mama June tries on a blond wig, marking the first appearance of Horny Bear. Sugar Bear finds a mullet wig that makes him feel smexy and ends up leaving the shop with it. Good times for all.

Shopping at the local department store

Dumpster diving. Namely, the Wilkinson County dump, where "you always can find a good deal." The family takes a trip to the "local department store," where they look for discarded treasures. They find everything from fans and speakers to toilet seats and mattresses. Alana is happy at the dump and suggests, "They should have a Dumpster Diva Pageant because I would win." Mama loves a good deal and nothing matches the deals you can find at the town dump!

Shorty Claus

This occurs when a man dressed as Santa Claus is much, much, much shorter than the ideal Santa Claus height. Mama June (and everyone in the town) calls Sugar Bear "Shorty Claus" when he puts on his Santa costume. Although he claims to be five foot ten, Mama June begs to differ: "You're lying, you're four foot eleven!" It doesn't matter—Mama June says the costume looks smexy on him and tells him, "You can wear that to bed." Ooh-la-la.

S'mage

A massage. When Alana and Mama June go to the salon for a spa day, they both get facials. Alana is looking to have soft skin for an upcoming pageant and Mama June wants to look smexy for her eight-year anniversary date with Sugar Bear that evening. After the facial (which Alana says makes her skin feel soft like a baby's bottom), Alana says, "I love s'mages! I can get a s'mage every day."

Smexy

Just the right combination of smart and sexy. When the family makes a stop at Shh! It's a Wig to find Alana a new wig for her upcoming pageant, they try on all types of crazy styles. Sugar Bear puts on a mullet wig and Mama June says, "Oh man, that is just smexy!" (Later on, Sugar Bear is seen leaving the shop with the mullet wig on, so he clearly thought he looked smexy too.)

Smoochie

A pet name for Alana, especially when she's competing in pageants. See also *Mootie Moot.* Mama June uses the nickname *Smoochie* when she's encouraging Alana during her competitions. (And, as Jessica says, Mama sounds just like a man when she's screaming it from the audience.) Alana says that all the enthusiasm from Mama can sometimes be a li'l distracting, because all she hears when she's performing is "*C'mon, Smoochie!*" Says Alana: "I mean, hello?! I'm trying to do a pageant here!"

Ta-dow

A jovial interjection that says something is finished, perfect, and there will be no further discussion. Mama June is fixing a Christmas tree decoration as Jessica stands by and taunts her: "Oh, it's goin' away now 'cause you just bursted that lightbulb. Sugar Bear, she just busted like three lightbulbs." Mama June replies, "As long as it lights up, it works, it's good. Duct tape or electrical tape. It works. Ta-dow." Jessica tries to knock the tree over by blowing on it, but June will have none of it: "Ta-dow. See? Leave it alone, it's perfect." Jessica replies, "Don't be 'ta-dowin' me," and Mama answers, "I will 'ta-dow' you."

Too-tay

That special part of a woman's anatomy, or another word for her rear end. We're just not sure! See also *biscuit, moon pie, pa-doose, va-jay-jay.* When Pumpkin asks Mama June why she needs to stockpile so much toilet paper through extreme couponing, Mama June says, "Because you need to wipe your too-tay!"

Tummy talkin'

Grabbing the vajiggle-jaggle around your belly button and squeezing it to produce the impression that your belly is talking. Alana is an expert at this and her tummy says, "Those judges were nuts!" (Mama June says, "Oh my God. Put that away.")

Un-nervouscize

To make yourself no longer nervous. When Mama June signs Alana up for a tap-dance class, she is a little, um, apprehensum at first, but she quickly gets her nerves under control and is excited for class. As Mama June says, "Alana's nervous at first and then she un-nervouscizes herself. And then she does a lot better." Later on, Alana helps Shugie un-nervouscize himself before a big event: "I get nervous for my pageants and I just shake it off, just shake it off."

Va-jaY-jaY

That special part of a woman's anatomy. See also *biscuit, moon pie, pa-doose, too-tay*. When Anna starts having pains in her belly, everyone is worried that her baby, Kaitlyn Elizabeth, is going to come into the world a li'l too early. They rush her to the hospital so she can be checked out, and the nurse sets her up on an ultrasound machine so everyone can see how the baby's doing. ("I got stuff on my stomach," says Anna. "That's called being pregnant," answers Mama June.) Anna is in a lot of pain and everyone is worried, and Anna cries, "Oww, it's going through my va-jay-jay!" In the end, however, Anna's va-jay-jay is fine and she goes home for several more weeks to await the birth of baby Kaitlyn.

Vajiggle-jaggle

Lumpy, floppy, fatty flesh exposed on a hot summer day that jiggles like melting Jell-O on the back of a pickup truck heading down a bumpy road toward the Redneck Games. As the Shannon/Thompson clan pull up to the Redneck Games in East Dublin, Georgia, they notice quite a number of very large and scantily clad women walking around. June is disgusted and comments that there are a lot of "broke-down people" out there. "Please, women that are of voluptuous size," she says,

"put some clothes on. All that vajiggle-jaggle is not beautimous!"

WoPsidEd

Not perfectly round. Uneven. The family picks out a pumpkin that Jessica proclaims is "wopsided," like Mama June's stomach. Mama June replies, "I'm not wopsided. I'm just curviness . . . and beautimous." The pumpkin is later destroyed when Uncle Poodle tries to wear it as a hat.

****

Pronounced "beeeep." See also ***, *****. We're not sure what this means, but it seems to come up a lot on *Here Comes Honey Boo Boo*. Especially when they have to get up early to go visit the farm: "All right, let's go, you all wanted to milk some ******* cows! . . . Let's go. **** this ****. Cock-a-doodle my **** ***."

Chapter 2

BE PART OF THE FAMILY

As long as we are havin' fun, makin' memories, together as a family, that is all that really matters.

—Mama June

Do you have what it takes to be part of the Honey Boo Boo family? Do you know your redneck name? Are you up-to-date on all Shannon/Thompson trivia? Can you differentiate fact from fiction? Finally, do you know exactly how to entertain your large, wild, and redneckilicious family no matter what time of year it is? Well, we have the chapter you need. Now that you know all the lingo, "Be Part of the Family" will take you to the next level of *Here Comes Honey Boo Boo* knowledge. You'll be so sassified that Mama June will be preparing a bed for you. Oh yeeeaah!

The Honey Boo Boo Name Generator

You can't be part of the Shannon/Thompson family without a crazy nickname, and luckily Alana has picked one out for you. You can find it by looking for the *Here Comes Honey Boo Boo* app on Facebook, or just follow the handy rules below. Are you a Raspberry Izzie, a Sugar Rumble, or a Sparkal Fluffy? Find out now!

1. Take the first letter of your first name and go to that section. Pick the word that best describes you. It's okay to be aspirational and reach for the stars (I'm looking at you, Crazy Morghan). So, if your name begins with "J," go to that section below to begin.

2. Take the first letter of your last name and go to that section. Pick the word that least describes you. Or just pick one that you think sounds good with the first name. It's okay, Alana doesn't judge.

3. Put them together and you've got your own *Here Comes Honey Boo Boo* nickname. For instance, if your name is Kate Robertus, you could be Kabob Roughhouser. If your name is Ernie, you could now be known as Enchantment. If your name is Joseph Vilain, you could be Juicy Vroom Vroom. But you definitely would *not* be Jeepers Raspberry—that would just be silly.

A

Adorable
Angel
Annie
Apple
Alana
Ava
Alicia
Aishlynn
Aardvark
Angel Boo

B

Blueberry
Blessed
Bunny
Beans
Boo
Boo Boo
Biscuit
Bug
Bear
Bliss
Booty
Booty Boo
Bloom
Beauty
Beautimous
Boo Bear

C

Chubbette
Crazy
Crackers
Chickadee
Crustie
Child
Cassidy
Cutie
Cutie Pie
Cookie
Candy Cane
Candy Candy
Cealy
Cereal

D

Door Nuts
Dirty
Dippy
Divine
Dainty
Daisy Duke
Diva
Darling
Dirty Ditty
Dumpling
Doodle
Doo-Doo

E

Effie
Eezy
Exuberant
Elmer
Elvis
Enchantment
Excellent
Eternal
Eccentric

F

Fair
Fairy
Fuchsia
Fluffy
Frosting
Forklift
Flair
Fannie
Farty
Flossy
Frilly

G

Grumpy
Goober
Glitz
Grace
Gum
Glossy
Grits
Goose
Gosling
Giggles
Grabski
Gravy

Glitzy
Gorgeous

H

Haley
Hammy
Heaven
Hayden
Harley
Holly
Hoo-Ha
Hungry
Hots
Hiccups
Honey Pie
Honey
Hooligan
Hon-Bun
Hubcap

I

Isabella
Impish
Inky
Itchy
Idjit
Izzie
Ice Cream
Ipsy Doo

J

Jinxy
Jazzy
Jasmine
Jayla
Juicy
Jabber

JoJo
Jalopy
Jackpot
Jenny
Jaclyn
Jeepers
Jadyn

K

Kennedy
Kiddie
Karmen
Kumquat
Kragen
Kabob
Kiwi
Kewpie
Kaleigha
King
Krunchy

L

Love
Lavender
La-di-da
Lacie
Lovebug
Lulu
Lovey
Luscious
Lala
Lipsy
Loafy

M

Mama
Magee
Mudslug
Mae-Mae
Mamie
Michaela
Moo Moo
Muffin
Morghan
Mini-Belle
Mary-Ellen
Meltdown

N

Noodle
Nita
Natural
Nanny
Nobby
Ninny
Nighty-Night
Nutty
Nutso
NoNo

O

Octave
Oasis
Ooo Ooo
Oinkie
Oinker
Oreo
Oyster
Olive
Orange
Ooo

P

Pageant
Peppermint
Presley
Poo Poo
Peanut
Paisley
Piglet
Pooh
Princess
Pumpkin
Piggy
Pennylicious
Precious
Pie

Q

Queen
Quaint
Quiet
Quick

R

Roo
Rump
Rascal
Roughhouser
Rumple
Rumble
Raspberry
Roo Roo
Radiance
Redneckulous
Raven
Rowdy

S

Smexy
Skylar
Supreme
Sugar Loaf
Spiffy
Sweetie
Sparkal
Silly
Sassy
Shoofly Pie
Shoo
Sugar
Sugar Bear
Sweetums

T

Teacup
Trouble
Tutu
Teeghan
Tony
Tantrums
Toots
Tan
Trixie
Tootie

U

Unbeatable
Unruly
Uncle
Uh-oh
Uh-huh
Upsy-daisy

Unpossible
Uncredible

V

Velma
Victoria
Vee Vee
Violet
Violent
Vroom
Victory
Vroom Vroom
Va-jay-jay
Very
Veronica

W

Weepy
Winsome
Wacky
Woo Woo
Whoa
Wiggly
Willy
Wiggy
Wisteria
Willow
Wicked

X

Xenia
Xena
X-Ray
X-cellent
Xeggs
Xexxy

Y

Yearling
Youngun
Yeti
Yellow
Yippee
Yolanda
Yellow Belly
Yahooooooo
Y'all

Z

Ziggy
Zealous
Zoe
Zippy
Zapper
Zany
Zoo Zoo
Zinger
Zabulous

Just remember you can't be Pumpkin. That nickname is taken.

The Honey Boo Boo Quiz

To be part of the family, you have to know everything there is to know about *Here Comes Honey Boo Boo*. Take the quiz below (or give it to a friend or family member) to find out how much Shannon/Thompson knowledge you actually have. Don't worry if you get some of them wrong—the family did too!

1. In the very first episode of *Here Comes Honey Boo Boo*, Alana claims each cheese ball you waste costs:

    a. 25 cents
    b. 50 cents
    c. 75 cents
    d. 1 dollar

2. Which sister does Alana describe as her BFF?

    a. Anna
    b. Jessica
    c. Pumpkin
    d. none of the above

3. When visiting the Redneck Games, Alana plans to participate in this activity:

    a. mud boggin'
    b. pie-eating contest
    c. dance off
    d. armpit serenade

4. When Alana needs to be cheered up after a pageant loss, the family:

    a. gives her a teacup pig
    b. gives her a chicken
    c. gives her a reindeer
    d. gives her a pep talk about how losses build character

5. During the trip to the food auction, Mama buys mainly this:

    a.   junk Food

    b.   MEat

    c.   baby supPLies

    d.   canned cranberry sauce

6. Couponing is an addiction that's even better than:

    a.   Food

    b.   gaMES

    c.   Holidays

    d.   SEX

7. Mama June says the girls will be happy to have this item stockpiled when the apocalypse hits:

    a.   canned souP

    b.   toilet PaPER

    c.   dEodorant

    d.   CHEESE balls

8. For Anna's baby shower gift, Alana makes the baby:

    a.   Painted wooden letters that sPEll the baby's name

    b.   a CHEESE-ball sculPture For the baby's Room

    c.   a mobile made oF little toy Glitzys For over the baby's crib

    d.   a Photo album Filled with Pictures oF the Family

9. Mama June and Sugar Bear go out on a dinner date for which anniversary:

    a.   FiFth

    b.   EigHth

    c.   tenth

    d.   none oF the above

10. As an anniversary gift, Sugar Bear gives this to Mama June:

    a.   sMEXY lingERiE

    b.   couPons

    c.   a golden dEER statue

    d.   a cookbook

11. Mama June got her forklift foot from:

    a.   a HORRIBLE disEASE

    b.   gEtting HER toE Run OVER bY a FORkLiFt

    c.   a tERRibLE mud boggin' accidENt

    d.   SHE was bORn witH it

12. When dumpster diving at the local department store, Mama June is excited to find:

    a.   a nEW soFa

    b.   an almost-usabLE sEt oF spEakERS

    c.   a bROkEn ligHt FixtuRE

    d.   a bRand-nEW toastER ovEn

13. At the Rock Star Divas and Dolls Pageant, Alana wears an outfit and performs a routine based on this superstar:

    a.   Madonna

    b.   FRank Sinatra

    c.   MicHaEl Jackson

    d.   ElVis PRESlEY

14. When the family visits a wig shop, Sugar Bear leaves the store wearing this style:

    a.   a MoHawk

    b.   a mullEt

    c.   a FaRRaH FawcEtt

    d.   an AFRo

15. Which sister claims to be a vegetarian?

    a.   JEssica

    b.   PumPkin

    c.   Anna

    d.   Alana

16. When they go out to a barbecue restaurant as a family, Alana wants this side dish to accompany her pulled pork and chicken:

    a.   a salad

    b.   macaRoni and cHEESE

    c.   Ribs

    d.   FREncH FRiES

17. When the family visits the beach, Alana has a chance to:

    a.   observe the lifeguard at work

    b.   swim with the fish in the ocean

    c.   help the vendor make hot dogs

    d.   all of the above

18. Which of the following is *not* a redneck word for that special part of a woman's anatomy?

    a.   moon pie

    b.   vajiggle-jaggle

    c.   biscuit

    d.   va-jay-jay

19. Sugar Bear takes Alana out for some father/daughter time to visit:

    a.   the circus

    b.   the Fun Factory

    c.   the movies

    d.   the county fair

20. At the end of the Guess Whose Breath? game, the definitive winner is:

    a.   Pumpkin

    b.   Sugar Bear

    c.   Anna

    d.   Alana

21. The family puts up a lemonade stand and sells each cup for:

    a.   1 dollar

    b.   25 cents

    c.   75 cents

    d.   50 cents

22. Mama June's number one favorite ingredient to use while cooking is:

    a.   deer meat

    b.   ketchup

    c.   butter

    d.   mayonnaise

23. Sugar Bear says the only time his family isn't talking is when they're:

    a.   SLEEPing

    b.   Eating

    c.   Mud boggin'

    d.   Farting

24. When Alana meets the beautiful Miss Georgia, she:

    a.   goES dRESS sHoPPing witH HER

    b.   gEts tiPs on PagEants

    c.   FaRts at tHE tablE

    d.   all oF tHE abovE

25. For Alana's seventh birthday, her sisters give her:

    a.   CookiEs, a bookEnd, and a nEw PEt

    b.   CHEESE balls, oRangE juiCE, and sPagHEtti sauCE

    c.   Hot sauCE, soaP, and PoP-Tarts

    d.   FancY Pajamas

26. When the family gets a group photo taken by a professional photographer, they decide to pose:

    a.   on tHE RoCks

    b.   in a Mud Pit

    c.   in tHE Pool

    d.   in a FiEld

27. When Alana gets new swimwear for an upcoming pageant, she says she looks like:

    a.   a cHunkY lEmon

    b.   a Pink FlowER

    c.   a bluEbERRY

    d.   a CHEESE ball

28. When Anna's baby arrives on the biscuit express, she's special because she has:

    a.   a conE HEad

    b.   no EYEbRows

    c.   two tHuMbs on HER RigHt Hand

    d.   all oF tHE abovE

29. Alana learns a new routine for the Sparkle and Shine Pageant from:

    a.   Uncle Poodle
    b.   Pumpkin
    c.   Nugget the Chicken
    d.   Miss Georgia

30. At the Sparkle and Shine Pageant, Alana wins this trophy:

    a.   queen
    b.   best swimwear
    c.   the people's choice
    d.   ultimate grand supreme

31. At the Troup's Farm pumpkin patch, the girls choose to ride out to the patch on:

    a.   a hayride
    b.   the cows
    c.   a tugboat
    d.   a car

32. When inside the corn maze at Kackleberry Farm, Mama June:

    a.   takes a phone call
    b.   cuts her finger and needs to find a bandage
    c.   gets lost for four hours
    d.   pees in the corn

33. For Halloween, Mama June dresses up:

    a.   as Marilyn Monroe, then changes to a mummy costume
    b.   as a mummy, then changes into a pumpkin costume
    c.   as Marilyn Monroe, then changes to a smexy vampire costume
    d.   as a pumpkin, then changes into a Marilyn Monroe costume

34. What did Sugar Bear throw to Pumpkin when he accidentally hit her in the eye?

    a.   a jar of mayonnaise
    b.   a set of keys
    c.   a handful of cheese balls
    d.   a can of cranberry sauce

35. After the family gives Glitzy the pig back to the breeder, they get a new pet. What kind of animal is it?

    a.   a dog

    b.   a Rabbit

    c.   a CHicken

    d.   a goat

36. When Alana says, "We're not animals, we're not a rabbit, we're people," what exactly is she trying not to eat?

    a.   salad

    b.   PEas

    c.   gRass

    d.   gRapes

37. At the end of their Thanksgiving meal, the family:

    a.   REFlects on How gREat tHE past YEaR Has been

    b.   gEts into a gigantic Food FigHt

    c.   wRaps uP tHE lEFtovERs to bRing to tHE Family acRoss tHE stREEt

    d.   givEs Mama JunE a PRESEnt FoR making sucH a gREat mEal

38. Jessica gets sick after eating as much as she can of which raw vegetable?

    a.   PotatoEs

    b.   BRussEls sPRouts

    c.   caRRots

    d.   collaRd gREEns

39. At Christmastime, the girls try to get Mama to kiss Sugar Bear by:

    a.   Hanging MistlEtoE

    b.   making a Romantic dinnER

    c.   sEtting uP mood ligHting using CHRistmas ligHts

    d.   PEER PRESSuRE

40. The family can't find a tree topper for the Christmas tree, so Alana decides to use:

    a.   Glitzy tHE Pig

    b.   onE oF HER PagEant cRowns

    c.   NuggEt tHE CHickEn

    d.   an oRnamEnt madE oF CHEESE balls

41. At the flea market, Alana buys this as a gift for Sugar Bear:
    a.   a FOUR-WHEElER
    b.   HAiR HEADS
    c.   SOME Hubba Bubba
    d.   a DEER statuE

42. When Mama June gets a gift she doesn't want, she thinks the best idea is to:
    a.   REGiFT it
    b.   SEll it at a YARD salE
    c.   giVE it to CHARity
    d.   RETuRn it FOR THE MONEY

43. Alana leaves this out on Christmas Eve for Santa's reindeer:
    a.   CHEESE balls
    b.   CARRots
    c.   tRAil Mix
    d.   COOKiES

44. Santa's reindeer leaves this out on Christmas morning for Alana:
    a.   a tHANK-YOu notE
    b.   a PRESENt
    c.   an autoGRAPHED SlEigH bEll
    d.   dEER POOP

45. During Christmas and throughout the whole year, the activity this family does that's the most important to them is:
    a.   going to tHE REDNECK GAMES
    b.   Visiting CORN MAZES
    c.   PlAYing on tHE REDNECK watERslidE
    d.   RAising MONEY and donations FOR CHARity

46. The most annoying part about living in Georgia is:
    a.   tHE HEAt
    b.   tHE tRAins
    c.   tHE gnats
    d.   all OF tHE abovE

47. What does Mama June say you should never buy at a flea market?

    a.   panties

    b.   wigs

    c.   headbands

    d.   food

48. Mama takes the girls' cell phones away from them because they:

    a.   refuse to go grocery shopping with her

    b.   will not do their chores around the house

    c.   steal too many candles from her secret stash

    d.   finish all the ketchup without telling her

49. If Alana ever became a wrestler, she says her name would be:

    a.   Little Miss Bling

    b.   The McIntyre Maniac

    c.   Silent Butt Deadly

    d.   all of the above

50. For Sugar Bear's forty-first birthday, the family gives him:

    a.   socks, a mug, and a new toolbox

    b.   pajama bottoms, a shaving kit, and a photo of Mama June

    c.   underwear, cologne, and chewing tobacco

    d.   a chocolate deer

51. . . . even though all Sugar Bear wants for his birthday is:

    a.   some alone time with June

    b.   some alone time with the girls

    c.   a four-wheeler

    d.   a chocolate deer

52. For Pumpkin's birthday, the family decides to:

    a.   visit a graveyard

    b.   stay at home and eat fried chicken

    c.   go to a barbecue joint to eat a four-pound sandwich

    d.   visit a pumpkin patch

53. What did Sugar Bear trade in to buy a ring at the pawnshop?

    a.   a turkey fryer
    b.   Alana's tap shoes
    c.   Jessica's boyfriend
    d.   a watch

54. Mama June's favorite phrase and philosophy is:

    a.   don't sweat the small stuff
    b.   it is what it is
    c.   you only live once
    d.   a dream is a wish your heart makes

55. According to Mama June, the most important thing in life is:

    a.   giving back to your community and helping others
    b.   being thrifty and feugel with your money
    c.   being with family and making memories
    d.   all of the above

Now check below and see how many you answered correctly!

Answers: 1 (b); 2 (c); 3 (d); 4 (a); 5 (a); 6 (d); 7 (b); 8 (a); 9 (b); 10 (c); 11 (b); 12 (b); 13 (d); 14 (b); 15 (a); 16 (c); 17 (a); 18 (b); 19 (b); 20 (c); 21 (d); 22 (c); 23 (b); 24 (d); 25 (c); 26 (a); 27 (c); 28 (c); 29 (a); 30 (c); 31 (b); 32 (d); 33 (a); 34 (b); 35 (c); 36 (a); 37 (b); 38 (d); 39 (a); 40 (c); 41 (b); 42 (a); 43 (a); 44 (d); 45 (d); 46 (d); 47 (a); 48 (b); 49 (d); 50 (c); 51 (a); 52 (c); 53 (c); 54 (b); 55 (d)

"Oh Yeah!" or "No Way!"?

Want to further test your knowledge of *Here Comes Honey Boo Boo?* Take a look at the following statements and guess which ones are true and which ones are not. If the statement is true, say "Oh yeah!" If the statement is false, say "No way!"

1. Alana started doing beauty pageants when she was six months old.

2. Pumpkin has never been the same since being hit by lightning.

3. When the family adopted Glitzy the pig, they put a baby playpen together for him to sleep in.

4. Mama June decided to dye her hair dark brown in order to have a new, smexy look.

5. Pumpkin was caught picking her nose at the local store and got kicked out.

6. Mama June learned to make multi-meals from Sugar Bear's late mama.

7. When Alana went in to get a new dress made, she asked the owner to make a dress for her pet teacup pig.

8. The family won $1,000 to spend on upcoming pageants by playing bingo together.

9. Mama June is afraid of mayonnaise because a babysitter made her too many mayonnaise sandwiches when she was little.

10. Sugar Bear is six inches taller than Mama June.

11. Mama June is legally blind, which is why she squints all the time.

12. Uncle Poodle got his head stuck inside a pumpkin at Halloween and couldn't get it out.

13. The family held a "Christmas in August" event to raise money and donations for charity.

14. Last year was Mama June's first time ever cooking Thanksgiving dinner at her house.

15. Alana's favorite gift she received from Santa Claus was a bicycle.

16. Alana says that the Christmas presents come from Jesus and Santa Claus delivers them.

17. Anna names her baby Catherine Rose.

18. The trip to the water park was the very first time the family had ever seen Mama's bare foot.

19. When they all went on diets, Pumpkin lost the most weight.

20. When the family got a new pet chicken, Alana named her Nugget after a chicken nugget.

21. Pumpkin thinks you can't eat marannaise and be a vegetarian.

22. Anna wants to be a lawyer when she grows up.

23. Jessica only brushes her teeth when her breath stinks or on special occasions.

24. Anna's baby was born with two big toes on her right foot.

25. When Mama June took the girls' cell phones away, she hid them in an empty butter container.

26. The family threw a surprise *Dukes of Hazzard*–themed party for Sugar Bear's forty-fourth birthday.

27. For Shugie's birthday, Jessica wrapped Alana up as a present for him.

28. Pumpkin would have gotten away with it if it weren't for those meddling kids.

29. Nobody in the family ever farts.

30. Mama June's personal credo is: "Do what I say, don't tell me what to do."

Answers

1. NO WAY! Alana was four years old when she started pageants.

2. OH YEAH! Pumpkin did get hit by lightning, which would be a life-changing experience for anyone.

3. OH YEAH! Although technically it was Sugar Bear who finally put it together.

4. NO WAY! Mama June dyed her hair blond, arousing the interest of Horny Bear.

5. NO WAY! Pumpkin hangs out there all day and they don't even make her wear shoes.

6. OH YEAH! June got the idea for multi-meals from Sugar Bear's mama.

7. OH YEAH! The dressmaker even measured Glitzy for a dress. But then the dress shop instituted a "no pigs allowed" policy. Talk about a mixed message.

8. NO WAY! They didn't win, and Alana thought that other lady was cheatin'.

9. OH YEAH! Mixing it up with some bologna might have averted a lifetime of suffering.

10. **NO WAY!** The television adds twelve inches.

11. **OH YEAH!** And even though she won't admit it, she might have seasonal allergies too.

12. **OH YEAH!** It was the worst version of "The Legend of Sleepy Hollow" ever.

13. **NO WAY!** The family did, in fact, hold this event, but in July.

14. **OH YEAH!** Next year she's going to work on the collard greens.

15. **NO WAY!** Alana's favorite gift is the television set.

16. **OH YEAH!** According to Alana, Elvis acts as more of a middleman between Jesus and Santa.

17. **NO WAY!** Anna names her baby Kaitlyn Elizabeth. And Kaitlyn Elizabeth is adorable.

18. **OH YEAH!** Next year Mama June is going to bring some aqua socks.

19. **NO WAY!** Pumpkin actually gained the most, which she said was her plan. But she might have been lying.

20. **OH YEAH!** Alana loves chicken nuggets because they give her nugget power.

21. **NO WAY!** Pumpkin correctly pointed out that there is no meat in mayonnaise.

22. **NO WAY!** Anna's career aspirations are yet to be revealed.

23. **OH YEAH!** Although she still has all her teeth, so she must be doing something right.

24. **NO WAY!** Anna's baby was born with two thumbs on her right hand.

25. **NO WAY!** She hid the phones in an empty cheese-ball container (naturally).

26. **NO WAY!** The family did throw this party, but for Sugar Bear's forty-first birthday.

27. **OH YEAH!** Jessica wrapped Alana up in tinfoil to give to Sugar Bear—best present ever!

28. **OH YEAH!** Alana and Jessica ratted out Pumpkin when she cheated at her bowling contest with Mama June. "Everybody's a snitch in this family," observed Pumpkin.

29. **NO WAY!** Unless there really is a fart ghost.

30. **OH YEAH!** Explains Mama June, "The kinda person I am is 'you do what I say' not 'you tell me what to do.' I mean, that's my personality. I'm always the big bitch in charge. That is very true."

Ten Essential Honey Boo Boo Family Activities, a.k.a. What to Do When Your Kids Are Bored

It's rough having four kids—especially on hot, sweaty, sloppy Georgia days when everyone is uncomfortable and complaining. But one thing nobody can accuse Mama June of is not spending enough quality time with her family. In fact, June has mastered the art of finding things to do with her kids that are both fun and affordable. As she says, "I have to keep the kids busy during the summertime. Especially Pumpkin. She'll be gettin' into some trouble and running the town." So what can you do with the family that's cheap but will also keep them happy and occupied? In this section, we will share some of Mama June and Sugar Bear's best secrets for keeping the kids entertained and happy. They've explored every option, from bingo, to setting up a lemonade stand, to building a redneck waterslide, to just sending them to the local food mart. So hee-haw, let's start havin' some fun!

1. Set Up a Lemonade Stand

Do your kids have a lot of energy? Is there something they've been wanting to save up for? Is it hot? Do you have some extra bags of sugar? Well, this is the perfect activity for y'all! To raise funds for a pageant, the Shannon/Thompson clan sets up a lemonade stand and makes a big batch of lemonade using Mama June's secret recipe. This was Alana's idea to make some extra dough, so it's something she's very excited about. After they set it up, Alana works the neighbors like any great businessperson, and she can barely keep up with all the customers who want to buy some lemonade. The family ends up raising $25 in only a couple of hours. This is the perfect activity to do with your family on a steamy-hot day, especially if they've been itching to have some change of their own. Here are a few ideas on how your family can set up their own stand.

TIP #1: Grab whatever you have around the house that can be used to make a sign—poster board, cardboard, markers, paint, glitter, anything. Make a large sign advertising your lemonade stand, saying how much each cup of lemonade costs. (Price your lemonade to cover all of your expenses, with a small profit included!) You might want to make an extra sign or two—when the Shannon/Thompson clan sets up their stand, you can see Alana standing on the side of the road holding an extra-big sign. She's also hollerin' like crazy to attract customers. That kind of enthusiasm will lure more people to the stand. Get the entire family involved, making posters and marketing the operation.

TIP #2: If you're a kid and the parents are buying the supplies for you, don't worry so much about how much the sugar costs. Let Mom and Dad cover your start-up expenses and price your lemonade competitively—maybe fifty cents a serving. Getting grown-ups to finance your adventures is a great skill to develop early. Remember, a dolla makes you holla!

TIP #3: Pick a place to set up the stand (such as on your lawn or the lawn of a friend who gets more people traffic) and figure out the time of day when the most people are out and about. Find a small table (anything will do) and a couple of chairs that are easy to carry and will fit in your chosen spot. Wipe everything down to make sure it sparkles and is ready to go when you open for business. This will be the glitziest lemonade stand ever created!

TIP #4: Now here comes the important part . . . use Mama June's secret lemonade recipe! (See "Honey Boo Boo Lemonade" on page 49.) Be sure to buy everything you will need to make your lemonade in advance. Pour lemonade into a couple of large jugs or pitchers filled with ice, and place them on a table where your lemonade stand is. Be sure to replenish the lemonade if there's a lot of traffic and you find yourself running low—you don't want to let down thirsty customers!

TIP #5: Scream your head off and wave signs like crazy to attract people. (This step is very important.)

TIP #6: Have a blast. Running a lemonade stand for a day or weekend can be an awesome family bonding activity and can teach the kids a little something about running a business. Plus, as the Shannon/Thompson clan has shown, you can actually make some extra dough. After your stand is closed for business, you might want to sit down together as a family (including pets) to discuss the experience. Or not.

2. Go Mud Boggin'

One of the things the family really enjoys doing together on a regular basis is mud boggin'. This is one of Sugar Bear's favorite activities. The family gets on four-wheelers in twos and threes (always wearing the appropriate safety gear) and plows right through mud pits, following each other and getting into mud fights along the way. Sometimes they also use black industrial inner tubes with the four-wheelers, which can be retro fun for the whole family. They attach the inner tubes to the four-wheelers and spin the kids all around, finally letting them loose into the mud pits. While this dangerous type of activity is not for everybody (just ask Sugar Bear's leg), basic inner tubes can be a treasure trove of fun and games for bored kids. You can find inner tubes at places like your local gas station, Target or Walmart, or online. They are fantastic to have at the beach, at the lake, or in the snow—or even just in the backyard for stacking and relay races, making a tree swing, or floating in a kiddie pool. Redneck fun at its very best!

If you want to try mud boggin' you'll have to find your own four-wheelers and a place where it's legal to drive them. In the South this is a sport you can enjoy year-round, and you'll probably know somebody who can help you get started. Otherwise you'll have to do some research and find both someplace where you can rent your four-wheeler and a place to take it out. Just remember to always follow local laws and always wear a helmet! And it's probably okay if you decide not to drive your four-wheeler through the mud.

3. Play a Rousing Game of Guess Whose Breath?

On days when the girls are feeling particularly bored and driving Mama nuts, they like to play a rousing game of Guess Whose Breath? together. You can't find a more redneck-ulous game than this one. One person sits in a chair, blindfolded, and one by one people come and breathe right in his or her face. The blindfolded person then has to guess the person depending on their different "fragrances," as Jessica says. In the contest that introduced the game to the world, Alana goes first, and when Jessica breathes in her face, she says, "It smells like A-S-S and it's Pumpkin!" She's wrong, of course, but then she says, "What does A-S-S spell, anyway?" When Pumpkin does breathe in her face, Alana says, "Pungent! It smells like booty-boo!" Pumpkin's turn comes up, and she nearly dies when Sugar Bear breathes in her face: "Eww! What did you eat?" At one point, Mama and Alana breathe in Jessica's face at the same time—great idea to throw her off! At the end of the game, it turns out that Anna guessed all five of them correctly while everyone else only got one or two right. And Jessica helpfully offers this information: "I'll be honest, I don't brush my teeth but on special occasions. Or my breath's stinkin'." If you and your family want to try out this now-classic parlor game, just grab a chair, a blindfold, and as many family members as you can. Take turns trying to guess each other's "fragrances." We can't think of a more disgusting way to get to know your family better.

4. Send the Kids to the Local Convenience Store

When the girls are feeling reaaaaally bored, Mama will let them head over to the convenience store right in front of their house. Pumpkin always walks over there completely barefoot (see "Bamm-Bamm look" on page 2). Alana loves to race around the aisles and try on items like glasses and goggles. Of course, the girls also purchase lots and lots of junk food. As one of the clerks says, "I think the store would go out of business if they didn't come there every day." Pumpkin likes to hang out at the convenience store the most and will spend an hour and a half there at a time. Sometimes Mama has to call over there to get the girls to come home. But the store doesn't mind at all—they lurve the family and look forward to them coming by almost every day. As the store's manager says, "The family adds a lot of flavor to the city of McIntyre." Getting to know your own neighborhood and being friendly with the locals is the perfect way to pass the time.

Everyone has a local store that is the center of their town's universe. Get to know the people who work there, and you'll always have a place to visit on hot days (and you'll maybe get some freebies here and there too).

TIP! Your local store may not be so cool with the Bamm-Bamm look. Start with normal footwear, then move on to flip-flops, and work your way up to bare feet over a few days. You'll be au naturel before they know it. Also, watch out for discarded gum. Gross.

5. Take June's Thanksgiving Quiz

Around the Thanksgiving holiday, June is sitting at the table with Alana and Pumpkin. June asks Alana what kind of homework she's doing, and she says she has to do a school project about Thanksgiving. Mama asks Alana what she knows about Thanksgiving, and Alana says, "Turkeys." Mama June says, that's it? What about the Pilgrims and the Indians? (As Alana says, "The Indians lost everything and just got a crappy meal. And casinos.") So Mama June decides to give Alana a Thanksgiving quiz, which Alana and Pumpkin both fail beyond miserably. For example, Pumpkin is pretty sure Christopher Columbus sailed the ocean blue in 1942 and that's Thanksgiving. Or maybe it was 1842? Anna is certain that Pilgrims are Amish people. Have you seen how they dress? Oh well—Mama June admits it's hard for even her to remember everything. So, since it's very important for the kids to be up on their history, you might want to try the following Thanksgiving quiz on your own kids. If they guess at least six out of the eight correctly, they're probably in pretty good shape! Fingers crossed . . .

1. The Pilgrims decided to hold the first Thanksgiving after:
   a. a successful harvest
   b. the end of a huge thunderstorm
   c. the marriage of two people in the community
   d. they first landed at Kribbit's Rot

2. The first Thanksgiving, in 1621, lasted:
   a. ten days
   b. three days
   c. one hour
   d. until they ran out of cranberry sauce

3. The first Thanksgiving was celebrated by:

    a.   the New England Patriots
    b.   the Pilgrims
    c.   the Mayans
    d.   the Amish

4. When the Pilgrims first arrived in America, they landed at:

    a.   Disney World
    b.   Kribbit's Rot
    c.   Bethpage Restoration
    d.   none of the above

5. Which Native American taught the pilgrims to catch eels and grow corn and acted as a general interpreter for them?

    a.   Squanto
    b.   Pocahontas
    c.   Stands with a Fist
    d.   Sits with a Squat

6. What year did Thanksgiving become an annual tradition?

    a.   1863
    b.   1969
    c.   1742
    d.   none of the above

7. Thanksgiving is celebrated on:

    a.   the second Saturday in November
    b.   the Fourth of July
    c.   the Fourth Thursday in November
    d.   all of the above

8. In modern times, a popular activity on Thanksgiving is:

    a.   Eating until you feel sick
    b.   watching Football
    c.   Hanging out with your relatives (perhaps mud-wrestling with them)
    d.   all of the above

Answers: 1 (a); 2 (b); 3 (b); 4 (d); 5 (a); 6 (a); 7 (c); 8 (d)

6. Buy a Cheap Backyard Pool

Sometimes, it just gets too darn hot. During the summer in Georgia, it can get to anywhere from 108 degrees to 112 degrees. During Fourth of July week, Sugar Bear decides to take some time off from work before school and pageants begin again. He buys a small backyard pool for the girls because "the more they're cooled off, the less they're nagging" him. Sugar Bear pulls out the instructions and gets to work, but Pumpkin and Mama say that he is terrible at putting anything together and hasn't done so in at least ten years: "Sugar Bear does not like puttin' sh*t together." But Sugar Bear works all day long putting the pool together, even as Alana can't stop bugging him to get the job

done faster. Finally, he is finished—woo-hoo!—and Alana jumps in even before the water in the pool has filled up. Sugar Bear predicts that they will break the pool in two months, although by the end of the day, it already looks like it is falling apart. If your family doesn't have a pool at home, think about buying a cheap one (even a small kiddie pool) for nonstop fun and adventure. You will be thankful, like Sugar Bear is, when the kids are cooled off and out of your hair. Just remember to always watch your kids around the pool so they don't get into too much trouble.

7. Build a Redneck Waterslide

If buying a backyard pool is not in your budget or doesn't fit in with your lifestyle, you might want to consider a super-cheap alternative—the redneck waterslide! This is an old thrifty favorite. Before the Shannon/Thompson family had a pool, they had to come up with some creative alternatives to cool down. (Washing your hair in the kitchen sink and wearing a redneck air conditioner can definitely cool you down, but both are pretty low on the fun factor.) The redneck waterslide is the perfect solution. One of the girls will go into the garage to find the tarp, and—presto!—instant fun. The girls lay the tarp down on the lawn and slather some baby oil and soap all over it. Eeeeeew! Then to make it reeaally slippery, they take out the garden hose and add a stream of water, being sure to make a big mud puddle at the end. Each person takes a turn slippin' and slidin' as Mama June keeps the water aimed right at the tarp. Yee-haw! When they all get tired of sliding around like crazy, they'll end up having mini mud-wrestling fights in the mud puddle. Then they all wash themselves off with the hose. As Mama June points out, "Rednecks take a bath, mud-wrestle, and waterslide at the same time." If you want to try this at home, all you need is a tarp, baby oil, soap, and water. Be sure to put a bathing suit on or wear clothes that you don't mind getting greasy. Be careful! These tarps can get more slippery than Glitzy in a mud puddle, but a great time will be had by your entire family. Be sure to mud-wrestle with your relative of choice at the end, and don't be afraid to fight dirty.

Indoor Version!

If it's too cold outside to make a redneck waterslide—or if you just want to make an enormous mess—you might want to try making an indoor redneck waterslide. To get revenge on Mama June for confiscating their electrical devices (i.e., phones) the girls decide to make their own version of an indoor redneck waterslide right in the kitchen. They wrap their bodies in garbage bags held together by tape ("new outfits"), rub the entire kitchen floor and everything in it with butter and oil, and start wrestling! The butter and oil (and garbage bags) make things slipperier than ever and the girls can barely stand up. They put butter on the bottoms of their feet and take turns running and sliding across the floor.

To make this at home you'll need a smooth floor—don't try it on carpet!—some garbage bags, and a lot of oil and butter. As Alana says, "More butter, more better, more slipperier!" But don't go too crazy—things take a turn for the gross when Pumpkin "washes" her hair with butter in the middle of the floor. "You know how long your hair is gonna be greasy?" says Jessica. It goes without saying that when Mama June comes home she is furious: "What in the hell are you all doing? This is what happens every time I leave y'all by y'all's self!" Jessica says, "Mama took our phones to have more family and sister time together, but all we did is get in more trouble." Have fun making your own butter/oil fiasco—whoops, we mean an indoor redneck waterslide—but just remember that someone is going to have to clean up the mess when you're done. Make sure it's not you!

8. Play Bingo with the Whole Family

You might think bingo is just for old people, and if you do you're dead wrong. Mama June loves bingo and often takes her family to the local VFW in Macon so they can all have fun playing it together. On one episode of *Here Comes Honey Boo Boo*, she takes them to play and she's hoping to make a little extra money to bring to one of Alana's pageants the following weekend. The family doesn't win at bingo very often, and the most they've ever won is $1,000, but June and clan are still hopeful that they will make the big bucks on this trip. Mama isn't sure if Alana understands the concept of bingo (dang, she asks a lot of questions!), but she hopes Alana will catch on so she doesn't end up having to play all of her cards for her.

Mama has been playing the game since she was ten years old: "They say it's an old person's sport, but I don't think so, I think it's very fun." She gets extremely intense about her bingo—bingo and couponing are her two favorite sports—and she ends up squinting a lot so she can see. This is called her bingo face. (Because Mama June is legally blind, she has that face on during a lot of activities.) June likes bingo because it's kind of like the lottery; you never know if you're going to win or not. When one woman starts winning a bunch, Alana has a theory: "That woman was cheatin', I'm not sure how, but that woman was cheatin'." Although they come close, at the end of the day the family doesn't end up winning anything and has to walk away empty-handed. But they bring all of their bingo supplies home for the next time (and there *will* be a next time!). Bingo is a super-fun game that the whole family can enjoy, especially if they've never played it before. Most towns have a family bingo night, so check your local listings for an event near you. Sometimes on family night, there are toys and games as prizes instead of cash, as well as pizza, balloons, snacks, and dessert. A great activity for the entire family to get into together. *Bingo!!!*

9. Take Your Daughter on a Date

Want to totally get rid of one of your daughters for the evening and also guarantee her a great time? Tell her father or father figure to take her out for some father/daughter QT. One time, realizing that he's been working a lot and worried that his girls are growing up too fast, Sugar Bear decides to take Alana out for a father/daughter "moment" at the Fun Factory. On the way there, Alana says to Sugar Bear, "I'm really looking forward to spending some time with you, just you and me," and Sugar Bear recalls the first time he saw Alana as a little baby. When they get to the Fun Factory, Alana and Sugar Bear go down slides, play arcade games, and jump into the ball pit. Alana collects a ton of tickets playing Skee Ball (so she can pick up a prize at the end). Alana and Sugar Bear decide to try roller-skating, and Sugar Bear asks if they have training wheels—even though he once worked at a skating rink! He can't even get the skates on himself and Alana properly. With training wheels in hand, Alana and Sugar Bear get out there on the rink and slip and slide all over the place, even going down for the count a couple of times. "My favorite part of spending the day with Alana alone is, I actually got to see her play and have fun, and she had a big smile on her face." At the end of the trip, Alana and Sugar Bear go to trade in their tickets for a prize. She chooses a big pink blow-up hammer. Alana and Sugar Bear have a great time, and Sugar Bear says he's going to try to do this more often in the future.

Nothing fights boredom and builds family bonding like father/daughter activity time. Plus, this gives Mom some time all to herself to do something on her own—like sleep or hit the local bar. So send your daughter off with Dad for the afternoon, or let them take part in a bonding activity while staying at home. Here are a few great things the two of them can do together *today*:

- **Make a meal together:** Sketti time! An awesome thing for fathers and daughters to do together is to prepare a meal. Even if it's just a lunch, your daughter will love planning and cooking a meal with you—and you don't even have to leave the house for this activity. Look through some cookbooks or look online together to find the recipe you'd like to make. Be sure that the planned dish is in line with both of your skill sets (mayo sandwich?). Purchase all the ingredients in advance, or go out together that day to buy them. And then get cookin'! You can even set the table together and make invites and menus. The possibilities are endless for this fun activity—and the rest of the family will benefit too in the form of a sit-down meal, since dinner always tastes better when someone else cooks it. If you really want to have redneck style, eat in the living room while watching TV.

- **Pick a flick:** Time for the jumbo popcorn slathered with extra butter! Kids and adults both love going to the movies, and sometimes a simple trip like this can be just the time together you need. Especially if it's cold and rainy outside. So if there's an age-appropriate movie that Dad thinks he can sit through, don't waste any time before heading off to the local cinema. And since this is a special trip for father and daughter, be sure Dad doesn't skimp on the goodies—soda, candy, popcorn with butter . . . cheese balls? Plan to do it up, and maybe even go somewhere to eat afterward so you can discuss the movie. As ordinary as it sounds, these are the kinds of activities that kids will have great memories of when they get older.

- **Wha?? Hiking?:** On the opposite end of the spectrum . . . get out there and enjoy nature together! Your town might have a national park or nature preserve close by that offers hiking trips with guides. Some of them are designed for very young children, some are for teens, and sometimes you can even bring your dog (or teacup pig). Check out the local offerings and pick a day and time to go together. Be sure to dress appropriately for the season, wear sneakers, and bring lots of bug spray (especially if it's spring or summertime). Not only is hiking educational for both father and daughter, since you're out there looking at all sorts of nature, but it gives plenty of opportunity for quiet conversation. Who knows what you will find out about your kid? Maybe that she hates lightning, dieting, or collard greens.

- Bodyslam!: Both Sugar Bear and the girls love attending professional wrestling events. As Sugar Bear laconically states, "Today we're going to watch wrestling and I'm so thrilled I can't contain myself." Anna is also a fan: "Wrestling is the best thing in the world, okay? I love it. It's my heart. It's my soul." The Shannon/Thompson clan already loves to wrestle, and they do it all the time at home (both in and out of the mud). "My family wrestles all the time in the house," says Alana. "That's why we love wrestling so much!" Pumpkin is even considering pursuing wrestling as a career: "I think being a professional wrestler may be coming in my future because I know how to throw people around and talk smack. *Yeahhhh*." So grab your daughter and take her to the nearest event. Make sure she practices her butt-kicking moves in advance and also rests those vocal cords so you can both chant, "Cup-A-Fart! Cup-A-Fart! Cup-A-Fart!" Alana's advice? "Always cheer for the good guys in wrestling."

   And even if one of your kids isn't so into wrestling, she might have a good time anyway. Mama June says, "Me and Jessica I don't think get into it that much." And Jessica agrees that there isn't much else to do but "look at the boys and eat." "There's some good-looking folks in there," gushes Anna. "Oh God, he's so good-looking!" But they might not smell that good after they've been knocked out by a Cup-A-Fart™ to the face.

10. Wash Your Hair in the Sink (a Redneck Shower!)

This is not as much an activity as a necessity, but washing your hair in the sink can be fun and can also cool you off! The bottom line is, not every family can afford a second or third bathroom. And the Shannon/Thompson clan is a very large family—with lots of ladies. (Sugar Bear is completely outnumbered and overwhelmed by all the females.) What do you do when there are five women and only one bathroom? Wash your hair in the sink! This saves precious shower real estate and definitely gets the job done. Also, as Mama June points out, it's better than taking a bath, where you just wash your hair in your own filth—yuck. Now, washing your hair in the sink is not as easy as it sounds, but with a little practice it can be quick, painless, and not at all messy. (Okay, well, maybe a little messy—but you can't be a real redneck without getting a little messy and muddy, right?) First of all, make sure you put whatever shampoo or conditioner you're going to use right next to the sink. This will keep you from running to the bathroom (possibly while someone else is already using it) with a head full of sloppy wet hair. Comb your hair out in advance and place a towel around your neck to avoid drips. If you have a detachable spray nozzle on your sink, even better! Use it to wet your hair thoroughly before lathering up. If you don't have a detachable nozzle, you might want to use a cup to rinse your hair. Keep the cup nearby and within easy reach. Lather up, rinse, repeat, and then use a conditioner if you want to. Use the towel around your neck to dry your hair so stray water doesn't fly everywhere. And presto! A nice, clean head of hair, with no bath necessary. 'Cause who wants to sit in their own filthy water?

Redneckulous Romance, Part I

Sugar Bear is not shy about showing his affection for Mama June or about his desire to see her dye her hair blond. He says: "Seeing June as a blonde would definitely make my loins perk up." And though June acts demure, she has a great sense of humor and can't help leading Shugie on. And grossing out her kids.

SUGAR BEAR: I'm in attack mode tonight.

MAMA JUNE: Aw pssshhhht. Frisky McBrisky. We don't do that kinda business in our house.

SUGAR BEAR: We can always go out in the yard.

MAMA JUNE: Never.

SUGAR BEAR: We got the back of a truck.

MAMA JUNE: No.

SUGAR BEAR: Throw a blanket down.

MAMA JUNE: No.

SUGAR BEAR: Under the moonlight stars.

MAMA JUNE: You are just over there daydreaming. You must be having some damn good dreams at nighttime because it sure ain't happening with me. You ain't got this in a while.

SUGAR BEAR: I wanna open that package back up.

MAMA JUNE: Pssshhhht. This package is sealed, delivered, and closed for business.

SUGAR BEAR: I can open it up.

MAMA JUNE: No. No.

. . . TO BE CONTINUED . . .

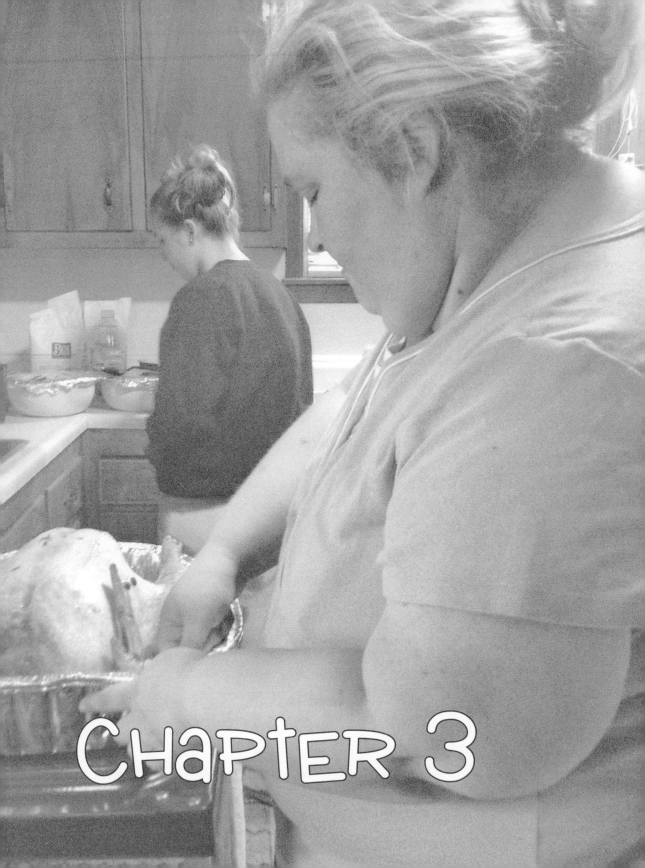

Chapter 3

JUNE IN THE KITCHEN

I'm not no Martha Stewart or, you know, Betty Crocker or anything like that. I mean, they have people that cook for them all the time. It's gonna be what it is and hopefully something turns out right and, uh, we can eat it.

—Mama June

No matter what she says, Mama June knows her way around the kitchen. She can turn roadkill into a family barbecue, can whip up some seriously sweet lemonade, and has a strong aversion to mayonnaise but a great fondness for cheese balls—the breakfast of champions! Money is tight, but thanks to extreme thriftiness, Mama June gets the family dinner on the table (or at least into a butter container near the couch) for the redneckulous price of $80 a week. In the next few pages, we will reveal Mama June's favorite family recipes and tips for feeding a large (and very hungry) family. From sandwiches to casseroles, you'll never again have to wonder what in the heck you should make for your own family to eat. So dig in and eat up, the Honey Boo Boo way!

SKETTI SERVES 6

One of the family's favorite meals is sketti, which is spaghetti topped with a tasty mixture of melted butter and ketchup. The sauce is a family tradition—as Mama June says, "The kids like the ketchup and butter, and I was raised on the ketchup and butter"—and can fill up an entire family for very little money. Alana loves to help her mom prepare this meal, making it even more of a family bonding ritual. "It's an old family recipe, don't tell nobody, Mootie Moot," orders Mama June. Of course, this dish is best eaten directly out of the empty butter container. How do you know if your spaghetti is done cooking? Throw it at the wall and see if it sticks!

2 pounds spaghetti

1 1/2 cups ketchup

1 1/2 cups (3 sticks) butter or margarine

Boil the spaghetti in a large pot according to package instructions and set aside. Place the ketchup and butter in a bowl and microwave until the mixture is melted. Stir, pour over the spaghetti, and serve. To make the most of this meal, sit together as a family in the living room while eating.

Ketchup Ain't Just for French Fries

Hey, we love us some ketchup! Ketchup is made from ground-up tomatoes mixed with vinegar and spices and was popular in the United States long before fresh tomatoes were a beloved fruit (or are they a vegetable?). These days, more than thirty-five million tons of ketchup are consumed each year in this country—and the culinary possibilities are truly endless.

Ketchup Soup: Mix ketchup with water and heat in the microwave.

Ketchup Dip: Mix ketchup with sour cream, Worcestershire sauce, and minced onion.

Ketchup Marinade: Mix ketchup with orange juice and soy sauce and pour over fish or chicken.

Ketchup and Potato Chips: Just open your favorite bag of chips and pour the ketchup right inside.

HONEY BOO BOO LEMONADE SERVES 20

When the family needs money for Alana's upcoming glitz pageant, they set up a lemonade stand and make a big batch using Mama June's secret family recipe. Alana can barely keep up with all the customers who want a taste of the family's tangy concoction. What makes it so special? "The secret to making good lemonade is a lot of sugar and a lot of lemon juice," says June. "I like a lot of sugar and stuff." Indeed, this special family recipe calls for two gallons of lemon juice and *five* pounds of sugar, making it as potent as potent gets. The recipe must be a real crowd pleaser, though—Honey Boo Boo and her family made $25 at fifty cents a cup in only a couple of hours!

2 gallons store-bought lemon juice

5 pounds sugar

3 to 4 cups water (optional)

ice

Mix the lemon juice, sugar, and water together in a big container and serve cold with ice. Get ready for the sugar rush of your life!

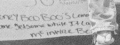

MULTI-MEALS SERVES 6

What makes a good multi-meal? "Just throw whatever you have available in the cabinets in a bowl," and presto! An entire meal for the family, all in one. Mama June uses her family as guinea pigs for these inventive concoctions, which always bring the entire clan together for sit-down dinners. (Although Anna will refuse to eat any multi-meal that looks like throw-up—and that's almost all of them.) Take a look in the cabinets and refrigerator and throw together any combination of meat, eggs, sides, or sauces that looks tasty. This is also a great way to use up leftovers before they go bad. When the ingredients are in the bowl—meat, sides, and sauce—be sure to mix it up with the best utensil available: your hands.

Breakfast

1 tablespoon butter

6 to 8 eggs, scrambled, or leftover scrambled eggs from the refrigerator

3/4 cup leftover ham, turkey, or bacon, chopped into small pieces

1 cup leftover mashed, boiled, or roasted potatoes,
cut up or fried into hash browns on the stovetop

1 cup shredded cheese

1/4 cup bread crumbs (optional)

Preheat the oven to 350°F, and grease a 9 x 13–inch casserole pan with the butter. Mix all the ingredients together with your (clean, washed) hands and transfer the mixture to the greased pan. If desired, crack in an extra egg or two and mix it all together again. Bake for 20 to 30 minutes or until the casserole begins to bubble. If desired, add extra shredded cheese and/or bread crumbs to the top and bake for 5 more minutes.

Dinner

1 tablespoon butter

1 pound chopped or ground leftover meat (chicken, beef, or pork)

2 cups leftover rice or potatoes (mashed or roasted)

$1/2$ cup shredded cheese

$1/2$ cup barbecue sauce

$1/4$ cup bread crumbs or fried onions (optional)

Preheat the oven to 350°F, and grease a 9 x 13–inch casserole pan with the butter. Mix all the ingredients together with your (clean, washed) hands and transfer the mixture to the greased pan. Bake for 20 to 30 minutes or until the casserole begins to bubble. If desired, add extra shredded cheese, bread crumbs, or fried onions to the top and bake for 5 more minutes.

Cranberry Sauce: Food of the Gods

"Cranberry jelly is the most perfect food," Alana says while playing with a can of cranberry sauce. "It's just the perfect color. Can shape is the most perfect food for eating. This is the food of the gods." It's a fact: cranberry sauce—also known as cranberry jelly—is almost certainly the mythical food of the gods, called "ambrosia" in Greek legends. Today, cranberry sauce is a delicious concoction of sweet red berries that has made the leap from Mount Olympus to our own Thanksgiving dinner. You can buy it chunky with the berries intact, or, as Alana prefers it, you can buy the cans that are filled with the delicious, gelatinous jelly that slides right out onto your plate and retains the shape of the can. In ancient legends, ambrosia conferred immortality on those who consumed it. These days the benefits of cranberry sauce are more modest. As Mama June says, "Cranberry sauce gets the fruit in their diet. It also makes sure their kidneys are flushed out and they don't get a urinary tract infection. When you got like, strong urine, they say, like, cranberry juice is good for that, so I guess cranberry sauce is too. So, it's like a win-win situation. They get their fruit, plus they don't get infection." Hercules could have done a lot worse.

TIP! You can eat your jellied cranberry sauce right from the can or slide it onto a plate and cut it into round slices. Mama June makes a cranberry-sauce lasagna by layering the slices on a dish with sugar. Food of the gods, indeed.

TUNA NOODLE
CASSEROLE SERVES 6

Mama June makes this dish at home all the time, and who could blame her? Nothing says redneck comfort food like that old-time favorite the tuna noodle casserole. The creamier, the better! Mama uses no less than six cans of tuna and one super-large can of cream of chicken soup in this dish. (As Mama June likes to say, "If it's not in a can, it's not for us.") Most versions of this classic recipe include peas, but since the Shannon/Thompson kids have a well-documented aversion to foods that are green, here we substitute Mama June's special ingredient, hard-boiled eggs. Be sure to mix the ingredients really well before pouring the mixture into the pan, and remember: "Your hands are your best utensils."

1 tablespoon butter

One 12-ounce package yolkless egg noodles

1 sleeve unsalted crackers, crushed

Six 6-ounce cans tuna fish

One 26-ounce can cream of chicken soup

1 dozen boiled eggs, chopped

$1/2$ cup 2% milk

Preheat the oven to 350°F, and grease a 9 x 13–inch casserole pan with the butter. Boil the noodles in a large pot according to package instructions, drain, and set aside. Spread half of the crushed crackers on the bottom of the pan. Mix the tuna fish, chicken soup, and eggs together with the noodles, and then add the milk. Stir the mixture and pour it into the pan. Bake for about 15 minutes. Add the remaining crushed crackers and cook for another 5 minutes.

HOMEMADE MAC 'N' CHEESE SERVES 6

This recipe is a real crowd pleaser because it includes no less than three huge-mongous hunks of different cheeses, as well as that all-American favorite ingredient: bacon. (See the recipe for GLT on page 58.) Mama and the girls like the cheese to be well done on top, so they bake this casserole for forty-five minutes. The end result is a bit cheesy-gooey looking, but no matter. As Mama June likes to say, "All that matters is that there's grub on the table and we're together. If it looks like crap, it's all right."

1 tablespoon butter

2 pounds elbow or spiral macaroni

1 pound American cheese, shredded

1 pound mild cheddar cheese, shredded

1 pound Parmesan cheese, grated

1 1/2 cups crumbled bacon, or real bacon bits

3/4 cup 2% milk

3 eggs

1/2 cup bread crumbs

Preheat the oven to 400°F, and grease a deep 9 x 13–inch casserole pan with the butter. Boil the macaroni according to package instructions, drain, and pour into the buttered pan. Add the cheese, bacon, milk, and eggs and mix it all together. Sprinkle bread crumbs on top and bake for about 30 minutes or until bubbly.

Cheese Balls: The Breakfast of Champions and So Much More

Ahh, that amazin' food group called cheese balls. First invented in the United States in 1930, cheese balls are extremely versatile and can be a great meal at any time of the day! The Shannon/Thompson clan has been known to eat them for breakfast. On the very first episode of *Here Comes Honey Boo Boo*, Alana grabs a tub of cheese balls to eat for her morning meal and spills them all over the floor. Mama June makes her pick up every last one and throw them in the garbage (instead of putting them all back in the tub). "We're just throwing away money!" says Alana. "It's fifty cents a cheese ball," chimes in Pumpkin. But Mama June insists her kids clean up after themselves and not act like little pigs (that's Glitzy's job). When baby Kaitlyn is born with two thumbs on her right hand, Alana says, "I wish I had an extra finger. Then I could grab more cheese balls!" And finally, on Christmas Eve, Jessica leaves a big bowl of cheese balls out for Santa's reindeer. Alana says, "I thought they liked carrots," and Jessica answers, "They don't know. They're orange. They can't tell the difference." Turns out, she's right—the reindeer eat every single cheese ball except for two of them. As Alana says, "Reindeer can't resist cheese balls. It's a known fact!"

ROADKILL BARBECUE

Waste not, want not! Salvaging edible meat off animals killed by automobiles is a thrifty tradition in parts of the United States. One day, the cops call Mama June to say that a deer has just been hit and killed. The family picks up the deer, names her Darlene, and then proceeds to make sausage in the garage. (It's always nice to name your roadkill before eating it!) As Sugar Bear says, "We love to get roadkill. And we like to clean it, grind it up, process it, put it in the freezer, and then on weekends we grill out and have a good time." But don't try this on your own at home—leave it to experts like the Shannon/Thompson clan! Below you can substitute store-bought pork for the fresh venison and make a sausage that is almost as delicious.

3 pounds lean pork, finely chopped

2 pounds pork fat, finely chopped

$1/2$ cup barbecue sauce (or ketchup)

$1/4$ cup ground black pepper

2 tablespoons salt

1 tablespoon garlic powder

1 teaspoon cayenne pepper

Grind the meat twice using a well-cleaned meat grinder. (You can also purchase pork from the store or the butcher that has already been ground up.) Mix all the ingredients together using a wooden spoon or paddle. Form the sausage into 12 patties. Heat a griddle or skillet over medium heat and cook the sausage patties, covered, for 10 minutes or so, flipping once. Uncover, raise the heat to medium-high, and cook for 2 to 3 minutes longer on each side, just to make the sausage patties crisp. Serve hot, and enjoy homemade sausage!

NOTE: If you want to stuff the sausage mixture into casings, you only have to put it through the meat grinder once. Sausages in casings keep better than patties, but both will freeze well if wrapped tightly.

COLLARD GREENS WITH BACON SERVES 6

While shopping for Thanksgiving, Jessica shocks everyone by requesting a vegetable. Namely, collard greens. "I don't know why I like collard greens," she says. "I'm not supposed to because they're green, but I just do." If you're not from the South, you may not be familiar with collard greens, which are sort of like a thick, bitter-tasting spinach. Mama June buys them but has no idea how to cook them, so she hatches a diabolical plan: she pits Jessica against Anna in a contest to see who can eat the most raw collard greens. The prize? Ten dollars. The girls eat the collard greens, even rubbing them with hog jowl (pork cheeks) to make them more appetizing. Jessica eats way more than Anna, but unfortunately, she promptly throws up, and so collard greens are off the Thanksgiving menu. Mama June confides, "Um, I didn't really want to cook collard greens so that was my way out."

If your kids want collard greens and you don't want to trick them into eating so many that they throw up to avoid having to cook them, don't worry! Here's a quick and simple recipe that will get the job done.

1 tablespoon olive oil

6 strips bacon, chopped

2 pounds collard greens, rinsed, trimmed, and chopped

4 to 6 cups water or chicken broth

Salt

Pepper

In a large skillet over medium heat, heat the oil and cook the bacon until crisp. Stir in the collard greens and add the water or chicken broth. Add salt and pepper to taste. Bring to a boil and then simmer until tender, about 45 minutes.

GLT (GLITZY, LETTUCE, AND TOMATO SANDWICH) SERVES 1

Okay, okay. We don't actually want you to use Glitzy! That would just be . . . wrong. It doesn't matter how redneckulous you are, it is still considered rude to eat your pets. (That's why you don't name an animal you plan on eating. We're looking at you, Darlene.) But no matter whether you're a redneck or a hipster or a guy who's had three heart attacks, everybody knows that bacon makes everything taste better. And what's better than the classic bacon, lettuce, and tomato sammich? This sandwich is extremely versatile and makes a great breakfast, lunch, or dinner. Plus, you'll be serving your kids something that's good for them: vegetables. Remember not to skimp on the butter!

3 or 4 strips bacon

2 slices white bread

Butter

2 iceberg lettuce leaves

2 tomato slices

Cook the bacon according to the package instructions and drain on a paper towel. Toast the bread and lay it out in front of you in traditional sandwich formation, one slice next to the other. Generously butter each side of the toast. Lay the bacon on one piece of bread. Top with lettuce leaves, tomato slices, and then the other piece of bread. Cut in half and serve. Yum, yum, bacon! (Just try not to think of poor Glitzy's relatives.)

Marannaise alert! A lot of people will want to use mayonnaise on their GLT sandwich instead of butter. That's a classic way to make a BLT and it will taste great—but it's completely up to you. Although Mama June demonstrates a crippling fear of mayonnaise in its pure, goopy form (see "Mayo-phobia" below), she says she's able to tolerate it as long as it's part of a dish—like chicken salad or, for instance, on a GLT sammich. However, if you're like Jessica and can't eat mayonnaise because you're a vegetarian, then skip the mayo and use the butter instead.

Mayo-phobia

Everyone loves mayonnaise! Well, most people. Mama June actually hates it with a passion. Mayonnaise is a creamy condiment that's made of oil, egg yolks, and vinegar. It was invented in France in 1756, but the first ready-made mayonnaise was sold in 1905 by Richard Hellmann at his New York deli. In 1912, he started packaging it in glass jars with the blue ribbon on the label that we all know today. Oddly, June will eat potato salad or tuna-fish salad if it's made by someone else, but she will not eat it if she makes it herself. She doesn't want to see the mayonnaise magic happening behind the scenes. Why is this? The answer: deep-seated childhood trauma. June once had a babysitter who gave her mayonnaise sandwiches for breakfast, lunch, dinner, snack . . . any ol' time! So, these days, June won't go near it. Pumpkin and Jessica think this is a ridiculous phobia. As Jessica says, "It's mayonnaise, it's white, and it's mayonnaise. C'mon. That's like ketchup, but it's just white." To try to cure Mama June of this phobia, Alana fills a big bowl with mayonnaise and puts it on the table right in front of her. You can "feel the tension in the air" as Alana brings the bowl in, and Mama feels like her throat is going to close up. "Mama was turning white, just like mayonnaise!" notes Alana. Unfortunately, Mama is not cured, but that's okay. Jessica won't eat *marannaise* either, on account of being a vegetarian. Besides, this family's number one condiment is and will always be ketchup.

MARANNAISE SANDWICH SERVES 1

Now we have the actual sammich that gave Mama June her lifelong fear of the creamy white condiment. Do you have the guts to try a marannaise sandwich? Although Mama June is deathly afraid of marannaise, a mayo sandwich is a longtime redneck favorite—it's definitely a guilty Southern pleasure. Just ask Santa's helper, Elvis! This recipe is super-delicious, easy, and cheap cheap cheap—all you need are two ingredients, the bread and the mayo. However, if you do want to take it to the next level, add thinly sliced onions to the sandwich. If you do add the onions, be sure to brush your teeth when you're finished. Unless you're getting ready for a game of Guess Whose Breath?. (Or if you're Jessica, of course.)

2 slices white bread

Mayonnaise, to taste

Thinly sliced onion, if desired

Lay the two slices of white bread in front of you in traditional sandwich formation, one slice next to the other. Take a deep breath. Approach the mayonnaise. Spread an ample amount of the creamy condiment on each slice of bread. Add some onion on one slice, if you like. Put the bread together and cut into halves. Gaze upon your marannaise sandwich. Enjoy!

Fryin' Makes Anything Taste Good

Although frying is always popular in the South, un-redneckulous Americans simply don't fry as much as they used to. But as any good redneck will tell you, anything fried tastes good! Any time you cook food in a good amount of oil, it's considered frying. However, what the following "Fish Fry" recipe calls for is deep-fat frying (when the food is immersed in the oil). No matter what type of frying you're planning on doing, here are a few tips that will improve the end result:

TIP #1: Does your grandma or dear ol' ma know how to deep-fry? Call her up and ask her to teach you. Then head on over, learn the ropes, and you'll end up with a delicious deep-fried meal. You'll also be preserving a secret family recipe of your own that you can pass on to *your* kids someday, and Mama or Grandma will be happy to see you. Now that you're ready to try it yourself, on to Tip #2.

TIP #2: Think about which oil you're going to use. Peanut and canola oils generally work best, because they have a high smoke point, so the food gets hotter with a crispier result. Corn oil will also work.

TIP #3: Have all of your equipment (tongs, thermometer, pot holders, and so on) out and ready to go before you start frying. This will make things easier when you're in the thick of it!

TIP #4: Try to keep the oil temperature between 350°F and 375°F. This is the best amount of heat for deep-frying, although you'll want the oil a bit hotter for French fries.

TIP #5: Never add too many pieces of food at one time (or the temperature of the oil will be reduced), and try to keep the pieces of food at a relatively uniform size.

TIP #6: Be sure to change your oil if there are any burnt pieces in it or if it's starting to smoke. This will make your food taste bad, and you don't want to end up with a bad batch.

TIP #7: Be careful around the hot oil and keep a good eye on it, especially if there are kids running around the yard. A watchful eye around the heat will save you a lot of problems later on. In the Middle Ages, they would pour hot oil on bad guys trying to invade the castle. Don't let that happen to you in your backyard.

FISH FRY SERVES 6-8

This family loves a good fish fry! What's a fish fry? A crazy-delicious outdoor feast with fresh fish, hush puppies, French fries, and anything else that can be fried in a deep fryer. You can set up a fryer right outside in your backyard, alongside a cooler of freshly caught fish. Be sure to have plenty of folding chairs so everyone can sit and eat together. Of course there should be bowls of cheese balls on hand too! Alana loves fresh fried fish and tries to stuff as much of it into her mouth at one time as she can, even as Mama June warns her to watch out for the bones. This recipe will show you how to make a fish fry at home, complete with French fries and hush puppies. If you've never used a deep fryer with hot oil, see the frying tips on page 61. This is a perfect summertime meal—or for any ol' time!

FOR THE FISH

6 to 10 whole fish, cleaned and scaled
(try catfish, bass, or red snapper)

Salt

Pepper

1 cup flour

Oil for frying

2 lemons, cut into wedges, for serving

Cut vertical slits in your fish to make them cook better. Salt the fish a little bit on the inside, and then sprinkle salt and pepper on top. Dredge the fish in flour. Heat the oil in a deep fryer to 375°F and deep-fry the fish for about 10 minutes or until crisp on the outside and cooked through. Work in batches and take care not to crowd the fish while frying. Drain the fish on paper towels and serve with a sprinkle of lemon juice.

FOR THE HUSH PUPPIES

1 cup cornmeal

$1/2$ cup flour

1 teaspoon salt

1 teaspoon sugar

1 teaspoon baking powder

One 8.5-ounce can creamed corn

1 large egg

$1/2$ onion, chopped

Oil for frying

Mix all the ingredients together. If the mixture is too dry, add a little milk or water. Heat the oil in a deep fryer to about 375°F. Working in batches so as not to crowd the hush puppies, drop heaping portions of the dough into the deep fryer and cook for about 5 minutes or until golden brown.

FOR FRENCH FRIES

6 to 8 potatoes, washed, peeled, and cut into fries

Salt

Oil for frying

Heat the oil in a deep fryer to between 375°F and 400°F. Working in batches, fry the potatoes for about 5 to 7 minutes, checking often to make sure they don't burn. When golden brown, remove and let the fries cool on paper towels before serving. Add salt—delicious!

CHUNKY PORK 'N' BEANS (A.K.A. BEANIE WIENERS)

SERVES 6

This dish is part multi-meal, part roadkill barbecue, and all delicious! One day, the family receives a roadkill alert in the form of a phone call—this time it's a hog that's been run over. Thankfully it's not a runaway Glitzy—this wild hog is about 175 pounds. "We're not really hunters in our family so when something gets hit around here they call us. Bring it home, free hog meat to fill up our freezer." The family drives to get the hog (chanting, "Hog jowl, hog jowl!" along the way), Alana christens it Logan, and then it's a family affair as everyone cleans and skins the hog together. Honey Boo Boo remarks that it's just like cutting cake. "People might think we're a little bit crazy when we come home and clean it and do it ourselves," says Mama June, "but why waste money at the store when we know that it's fresher and cleaner on the side of the road?" The family brings the meat home and bakes every part of Logan with beans—even the feet, tail, and snout. It's a favorite in the Shannon/Thompson household, Mama June says: "You kill it, you put it in some food . . . when it's cooked you'll love it."

If you don't have access to a whole hog or aren't comfortable processing the hog yourself—Jessica says the worst part is the smell—try this version, which substi-

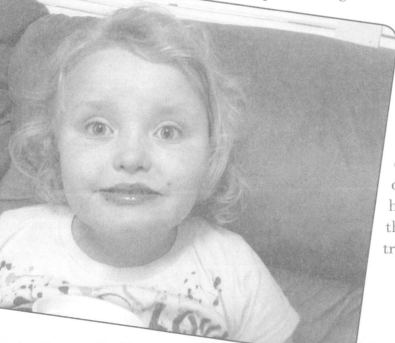

tutes weenies for the snout, tail, and trotters. Be sure to mix it all up with your hands before baking!

1 tablespoon butter

Six 8-ounce cans baked beans

16 hot dogs

6 strips bacon, cooked and crumbled

1 cup brown sugar

Preheat the oven to 350°F, and grease a 9 x 13–inch casserole pan with the butter. Open the cans of beans and pour them into the casserole pan. Add the hot dogs, whole, and bacon, and mix everything together with your hands. Sprinkle brown sugar on top and bake for about 20 to 25 minutes, or until nice and bubbly.

Chapter 4

EXTREME COUPONING, FOOD AUCTIONS, AND OTHER WAYS OF SAVING YOUR DOUGH

Couponing is a serious addiction. It's even better than sex.

—Mama June

It seems downright impossible, but Mama June feeds her large family of six on $80 a week. How the heck does she do this? The Shannon/Thompson family loves to eat, and roadkill doesn't grow on trees (although it often ends up hanging from them). It's all about being resourceful, thrifty, and feugel, and in this chapter, we'll show you some of the ways that Mama June is able to save some money, which she puts aside for pageants and other nice things for the family. Through "extreme sports" like couponing and taking part in local food auctions, Mama's family is never in need of anything—especially not toilet paper. Here are some of Mama June's best tips, tricks, and ideas for getting that extra dolla that will make you holla. Extra money is a beautimous thing!

The Coupon Queen's Guide to Couponing

One way that Mama June is able to afford the pageants, which can cost thousands and thousands of dollars, is by couponing. That's why June is known as the Coupon Queen! By couponing, you can potentially cut 80 percent or more off your normal grocery bill and leave the grocery store with a lot more items for the money. Incredibly, you can even get many of these items for free. *Free!* It all depends on you being organized with your coupons, doubling up (or stacking), and staying on top of deals. You'll have plenty of dough left over for all the glitz pageants you want. Maybe you'll even be able to buy a matching dress for your pet teacup pig.

Couponing can seem intimidating if you have never done it before. How do you do it? Do you cut the coupons out or just leave them in the flyer? Do you stick the coupons on the fridge and then never look at them again? Are the clerks at the store going to yell at you when you pull out an enormous wad of coupons? What's with this whole "Internet" thing? It does take some time and effort, but with a little work and practice you'll get it right. As Mama June says, "I taught myself, so it's not that hard. It doesn't take a rocket scientist to coupon."

Mama June has always been feugel, but where did she get the idea to start couponing? The answer: through word of mouth. Some of the moms she became friendly with through the pageant circuit were talking about couponing and

June's ears perked up when she heard about how much money they were saving. In fact, many of these moms were bragging on social media (you know the site) about getting their items for free. *Free!* June was so impressed (and, of course, intrigued) that she started asking the other moms how they did it. "If they can do it, I can do it too!" she said. And do it she did. June quickly scored some great deals: one time, she bought a thousand boxes of crackers for only $33 using coupons! (She basically only had to pay the sales tax.) And if you watch the show you can see for yourself June's success in securing an apocalypse-proof supply of bathroom tissue. Couponing is now an everyday part of June's life, and if you too are interested in using more coupons at home, here are some of Mama June's best tips for getting started.

TIP #1: Go extreme! Collect as many coupons from newspapers as you can, but don't just stop at one newspaper. That's for amateurs! Check out as many weekend papers as possible or ask for the enclosed flyers from friends and neighbors who aren't using them. Double up on the coupons as you're collecting, meaning it's okay to have more than one of the same coupon. The more coupons you have, the more money you will save. And don't forget to use the coupons that are provided to you by the stores where you shop—Mama June watches the sales very closely at her local store. Also, in the past, Mama June has found great coupons in the free newspapers that are stacked next to ATM machines, so be resourceful and don't forget to look in every nook and cranny.

The goal is to find coupons that are stackable, meaning that you can use a manufacturer's coupon with a store coupon. If you can stack those on a day when the store is having a sale, you might be in for a real bargain. You may even be able to score some super-cheap Chef Boy Bar Dean.

TIP #2: Get organized! Find a way to order your coupons so you don't lose track of what you have. You can organize them by expiration date or by item—whatever works best for you. Mama June keeps a big binder at home with tabs, and she sorts her coupons by the type of food or grocery item: raisins, frozen foods, dish detergent, etc. You can make sections for whatever items are important to you and your family. For instance, you might have a separate section just for hog jowl. Then take some time before you go shopping to review your coupons, and also decide how much money you'd like to spend total. You can take the entire binder to the store with you, or you might choose to buy a small coupon organizer that you can keep in your purse.

If you're heading to a new store, you also might want to look up the store's coupon policy. Knowing in advance what the policy is might save you time if there is a problem while checking out. Putting in the time beforehand is going to save you time and money in the checkout line. (And the quicker you get home the sooner you get to eat that delicious hog jowl.)

TIP #3: Go online! Most people only use the Internet to goof off, so they never think to look for coupons there. But trust us—you can find some great deals. Lots of websites offer printable coupons or promotion codes that you can use, sometimes in conjunction with other coupons. Some popular couponing websites include Groupon.com, Coupons.com, SmartSource.com, and SlickDeals.net, but there are many others available.

TIP #4: There's an app for that! If you have a smartphone or other electrical device, there are some fantastic apps available to help you find coupons. One of the most popular is Coupon Sherpa, which helps you find available coupons for almost every store out there. You can search for a particular store or scan categories such as "health and beauty," "clothing," "pet supplies," and "home and garden." Since your phone is always with you (unlike your coupon binder), it's very difficult to miss any savings with this handy app. Again, you'll want to check which coupons are stackable when you're planning your shopping strategy. If you can't find your electrical device, check the empty cheese-ball jar on top of the refrigerator.

TIP #5: Be patient. As Mama June says, don't be so quick to use a coupon as soon as you get it. It's okay to save it for later, just like the family saved roadkill hog Logan for later by sticking his butchered parts in the freezer. Finding the right time to unleash your payload of stacked manufacturer and store coupons can make all the difference. Pay attention to the sales at your local store. Sales repeat themselves every six weeks, so almost everything will go on sale again very soon. If you use your coupon right away, you will only get the money off that the coupon says. However, if you use the coupon on a sale item, you will get the coupon amount plus the sale amount off. Patience definitely pays off in the coupon game, so stick those coupons in the freezer right next to Logan's hog jowl. But just remember: even though Logan is frozen, he won't stay good forever, and neither will your coupons. Keep an eye on the expiration dates so your coupons don't expire before you can use them.

TIP #6: Stockpile for future use! A big part of couponing is stockpiling items, since only certain items go on sale at one time. For instance, the best time to buy Halloween candy is right after Halloween. Then you can pack it up and put it in storage for next year. Everyone knows candy never goes bad. Mama June is an expert at stockpiling items for the future—she neatly lines up rows and rows of dish detergent, laundry detergent, toilet paper, and snack items on shelves in the dining room. And in some of the hallways. Mama June is not only great at stockpiling for the regular future, she's also planning for the special postapocalyptic future. "When the apocalypse hits at the end of the year—they claim it's gonna hit—I could sell that roll we got for free, your toilet paper, for freakin' five hundred dollars," says June.

Be aware that there are often more coupons for "staple items," as June calls them, than there are for real food. But if you stockpile these staple items through couponing—soaps, shampoos, deodorant, laundry detergent, etc.—then you will have more money available to buy fresh fruit, vegetables, and meat for your family meals. And you'll have more staples to sell should the apocalypse hit. (Mama June is also a big fan of candles, so she buys a lot of these when they're on sale and stockpiles them for future use. There's always a candle burning in her house, thanks to couponing! Although Mama June doesn't seem particularly impressed when Sugar Bear lights some to be romantic.)

Before you begin stockpiling, take a good look at your house and decide how much room you have to play with. Make sure your family is aware of what you're going to do and that they all know that a certain part of the house will be reserved for stockpiled items. The lucky Shannon/Thompson girls get to dine every single night while surrounded by toilet paper, salsa, and dish detergent! Or at least they would if they didn't eat on the couch every night . . .

TIP #7: Devote time to your new hobby! If you want real savings, you need to put aside time to work on cutting coupons and reading sale flyers. As seen on *Here Comes Honey Boo Boo,* Mama June spends a good amount of time at the kitchen table, cutting out and organizing coupons. Sometimes her girls are with her, so they can see what she's doing and get involved. The more time and effort you put into it, the more savings you'll have at the end of the day. Time is money, and extra money is beautimous.

Now take all these extremely simple and concise tips and put them into action! In no time at all you'll be saving big money and have an enormous stockpile of toilet paper and hair products!

Feeling a little overwhelmed? Here's an example of a real-life shopping trip where Mama June puts her couponing strategies to work. On an early episode of *Here Comes Honey Boo Boo,* Alana is preparing for a new pageant where she will need an expensive new wig and an expensive new glitz dress. Mama June sits down with the girls to amp up her couponing in order to save money for the pageant necessities. June decides in advance that she wants to spend about $20 on this trip, and she is definitely going to buy more toilet paper. Alana points out that June already *has* a whole bunch of toilet paper in the pantry (Anna says, "If there was a world disaster at our house, and the whole entire America has to come to our house, we'll still have toilet paper left over"), but Mama June wants to buy anyway, because with the coupon it will be free. *Free!* ("Every time I go into the store people think that I have a bowel movement problem, but the reason why I have so much toilet paper is because it's free. Hello!") After getting to the store, Mama June finds some of the following deals:

14 chocolate bars = FREE (with coupon)
10 packages of ramen noodles = FREE (with coupon)
Mustard = 89 cents (with coupon)

At the end of the trip, the retail value of everything she buys is $132 and she pays only $27.40! Her total savings through couponing is $102 that day. She doesn't quite meet her goal of spending $20, but she comes very close. And she does it through planning, organization, and lots of cut coupons. Smexy!

Thanksgiving offers another great example of extreme couponing in action. To prepare for the feast, Mama June takes Alana, Anna, and Jessica to the grocery store with her to go shopping. The morning paper had some very nice sales, and she takes the three girls so she can continue to teach them the art of saving their money. Mama June is very impressed when Jessica finds some crackers with a coupon attached to them. And then Mama walks Alana through figuring out how much money they will save when they buy the "buy one get one free" canned-corn selection. As Mama says, "Off-name brands are sometimes better than name brands." ("No, not really," replies Pumpkin. "Not like beef raviolis like Chef Boy Bar Dean.") Jessica likes collard greens, so the family buys a huge bunch of those, even though Mama June doesn't know how to cook them. They also find Alana's favorite: jellied cranberry sauce (a.k.a. the food of the gods) for Thanksgiving Day—twenty-four cans to be exact! They end up saving a lot of money and Thanksgiving is done and bought, making Mama June very happy. But Mama June isn't done yet. She also comes up with a plan to avoid having to cook the collard greens by pitting Anna against Jessica in a collard-greens-eating contest. The girls rub hog jowl on the greens to make them tastier, but it doesn't help. In the end, Jessica throws up and the collard greens are wasted, but

Mama June is happy because she doesn't have to cook them. Technically you might think that Mama June wasted money by buying the collard greens and not cooking them, but we think you'll agree that watching the kids eat them till they made themselves sick more than makes up for the cost of the purchase. Mama June wins again.

Local Food Auctions

Auctions aren't just places to buy foreclosed homes, distressed properties, or speedboats that have been seized by the police. They're also great places to buy slightly damaged or close-to-expiring food! And you can buy it in bulk! The weekly food auction is another way that Mama June budgets and saves money. In fact, it's one of her favorite activities. Food auctions are a lot like the other kinds of auctions that you've heard about, except they are aimed at people looking for items they'd get at the grocery store, not people looking for storage units full of old newspapers. Food auctions sell off perfectly good items that supermarkets or food distributors are trying to get rid of. These grocery items are sold at a deep discount, making them perfect for a large family on a budget. Most of the food (and even some paper goods) that is sold at auction is either dinged up, slightly damaged, or nearing the expiration date—but the food is perfectly safe and possibly even delicious! June goes there once a week and brings the entire clan. Mama June explains, "I'm a thrift-saving mommy, so we save a little bit of money that way." They stock up on cookies, cakes, chips, pasta, bread, and anything else that looks tasty. (Although Alana wants a lot of sweets and cakes, and Mama June has to remind her, "They're not good for our diet!" "He had some good stuff, though!" says Alana.) At the local food auction, June ends up paying about a third or less of what she would have paid at the grocery store. "I know some of it is close to expiring," June says, "or maybe fell off the back of a truck, but pssshhhht, it's cheap." If you'd like to give this a try, keep the following in mind:

TIP #1: Food auctions often mean buying in bulk; you can purchase a large number of items for very little money. As with couponing, take stock of your house and make sure you have space to store all the items. Be certain that your family knows where the stash is and that they can't dip into it at will. (We're looking at you, Pumpkin!) You might have to exercise some restraint—a crate of fat cakes direct from the fat-cake factory is very tempting, but do you really need that many? You probably do, so don't let someone else win that auction.

TIP #2: Search online to find grocery auctions in your area, or visit the National Auctioneers Association (Auctioneers.org). When you find an auction that looks interesting, call in advance to find out which method of payment they take, whether you need to register, if wearing shoes is required, and any other details you need to know about in advance. If you can't find an auction in your area, there are wholesale grocery sites online where you can bid for items over the Internet.

TIP #3: Get organized. As with couponing, spend some time getting yourself organized in advance. Decide how much you'd like to spend total and make a list of groceries that you'll be looking out for. Do you have a place for the mega-size box of fat cakes that you will soon purchase? Where will you put the extra hog jowl? Taking some time beforehand will curb excessive spending and impulse purchases (such as those sponge-cake shells that Alana just had to have!). If you've already started couponing, you should have an idea of what's a good deal and what isn't—this will come in handy as you bid for various items.

TIP #4: BYO containers. Food auctions usually don't provide grocery bags, so be sure to bring plenty of boxes and coolers so you can carry your newly won treasures home and so the food won't spoil while you're finishing up your auction. Pack more containers than you think you'll need, especially if you can't follow Tip #3 and you're an impulse shopper.

Other Ways of Saving Dough, a.k.a. Redneck Shortcuts

On *Here Comes Honey Boo Boo*, couponing and grocery auctions aren't the only ways the family saves money. Mama June finds all kinds of ways to save, some big and some tiny. No stone is left unturned! Here are some of the shortcuts and tricks the family has employed to save some money:

DIY, Y'all!

In one episode, Mama June decides she's going to try to learn to do Alana's hair and makeup for pageants so she can save $300 to $400 per event. This will result in big savings for the family! Mama June arranges to have a step-by-step tutorial at the local salon so she can see if she can do it like the pros. The hair and makeup stylist, Jennifer, says she's going to do half of Alana's face while Mama June does the other half. Jennifer walks Mama June through as she makes up her half of Alana's face and then turns Alana over to Mama so she can work her magic. Unfortunately, June has a little problem with her eyesight (she even had trouble locating Alana's eyebrows), so she made Alana look like a bit of a rodeo clown. As Alana says, "Mama, it looks like you squished a marshmallow on my face!" While this maybe didn't work out as well as planned, it's a great idea to teach yourself how to do things you often pay a lot of money for. Not only does this result in big savings, but it can be fun to learn a new skill. (Also see "Mani-Pedis June-Style" on page 94.)

Speaking of DIY, this also applies to the redneck waterslide! When the family needed some way to cool off in the yard and they didn't have a waterslide, they created one of their own in the backyard (see page 38). But there are all kinds of things you can do in your yard that cost absolutely no money. Set up a sprinkler and then arrange inner tubes for relay races. Hide coins (or cheese balls) throughout the yard and send the kids on a red-neck treasure hunt. Fill leftover birthday party balloons with water and host a neighbor-hood water-balloon fight with the sprinkler running. Or pick a night for the kids to grab their sleeping bags and camp out under the stars. All cheap, redneck, DIY fun!

Too hot out there? Don't forget the redneck air conditioner! Take a cool, wet towel and wrap it around your head on mega-hot days. This is perfect for the beach or sitting in the backyard while watching the kids play. You don't have to spend a lot of money to cool down!

Flea Market Madness!

At Christmastime, Mama June takes the family to a flea market to purchase gifts. "A flea market is a bargain shopper's best friend," Mama June says. "One person's junk is another person's junk!" says Alana. Mama June gives each of her girls a budget of ten dollars but tells them to try to spend less than that if they can. This is a great way of teaching the family the value of a dollar. Pumpkin finds some adorable—but used—underwear, which Mama doesn't approve of: "You don't buy panties from a flea mar-ket!" "That's a Pumpkin gift," says Pumpkin. Alana tries to find Sugar Bear some shoes, but she can't find any in his size, so she settles for two wig heads with real hair (or as she calls them, "hair heads"). Since Sugar Bear likes to run his fingers through Mama's hair, Alana reasons that he will love these two heads, which she names "Iris One" and "Iris Two." "Shugie likes to run his hand through Mama's hair so he's gonna love my gift," says Alana. "My Sugar Bear loves to play with . . . stuff like this. This would be a good gift for him." Visiting flea markets is a fun activity for the entire family and you can find great bargains. It's also a great place to start teaching your kids how to manage money and a budget. Find your local flea market by checking the newspaper or search-ing online, but be sure to get there early, before all the good items are taken!

Alana is just a normal kid who loves her friends, loves her family, and hates vegetables. And no matter what, she's always sassified.

Honey Boo Boo's *Photo Album*

The local food auction is a great place to stock up on staples and save some money for the upcoming glitz pageant. Just don't tell Jessica you bought the fat cakes.

Mama June and Sugar Bear. As Mama says, "Was it love at first sight? No. Was it bed at first sight? Maybe. You gotta try the milk out before you buy the cow . . ."

Mama and Alana, hangin' in front of the house. As Alana says, "Pretty comes in all different sizes. My size is cute!"

Mama June and a sassified Alana discuss the finer points of preparing dinner. **Mo' butter, mo' better!**

Fun day at the water park. "Mama, this life jacket makes me look like a chunky lemon!" Mama replies, "It does . . . it makes you look beautiful."

Mud boggin' with the whole family (with helmets on, naturally). Alana says, "I like to get dirty like a pig!"

Family values. This crew just likes to hang out together and have fun. Because as Mama June says, "If you're not having fun, then why do it to begin with?"

Sugar Bear puts the backyard pool together. Even though traditionally "Sugar Bear does not like puttin' sh*t together," he makes an exception so the kids can cool off during the hot Georgia summer.

The local wig shop: where smexy and beautimous meet. The family had a great time and Sugar Bear first discovered he liked June with blond hair.

Alana at the Fun Factory. Sugar Bear says, "My favorite part of spending the day with Alana alone is, I actually got to see her play and have fun, and she had a big smile on her face."

Alana meets baby Kaitlyn Elizabeth for the first time. "Baby Kaitlyn is so tiny . . . I POOP bigger!"

On an outing to Troup's Farm to pick out pumpkins, the girls opt to take the cows to the patch, while Mama hitches a ride in the pickup truck.

Alana says, "I think baby Kaitlyn is going to be the best nose picker in the whole entire family."

Carving your pumpkins outside keeps the disgusting mess out of your house. "As soon as I realized that the insides were such a gooey mess, I knew we were in big trouble," says Sugar Bear. "They just like getting messy, that's all."

The Shannon/Thompson clan gets their scare on.

When Alana's not going to school, scouting, or hitting the pageant circuit, she's doing the things every other little girl in America likes to do . . . like riding horses.

The family at the start of a beautiful Thanksgiving feast. As Mama says, "The best part of Thanksgiving is just being with my family and makin' memories. That's what it's all about."

. . . and the best part of eating outside is not having this mess in your house.

The family together.
It is possible to take
a photo without
someone farting.

Alana and her BFF, Glitzy the teacup pig. She had big dreams for Glitzy: "We're gonna make you a pageant gay pig."

Regift!

One of the ultimate redneck quick fixes is the regift. Why spend time and money buying a present when you can just give the person something you've already received but didn't really want? Mama June says, "I really hate taking stuff back, exchanging it. So if I get something I don't want, it's getting regifted." Just save up all the unwanted presents you receive and store them in one place, so you can easily find them when the time comes that you need a present. If you're really on the ball, you may want to attach a tag to the present noting when you received it and who from, so that you can pull off the

Ultimate Regift (see next page). Mama keeps all of her regiftable items in her closet, and one day Alana sees her going in there and asks what she's doing. Mama June says she's trying to find a present for Uncle Poodle. Alana says, "Why don't you just buy Uncle Poodle a present?" and Mama June answers, "I have too many things to regift that I'm not gonna waste money on Uncle Poodle." Mama explains her basic formula:

GIFT + TIME = REGIFT

"It's simple math," says Mama June. "Save money, and also regifting is what you call free." Mama is all about not spending money out of her pocket, and she's proud of it. As Jessica says, "Mama, you're just cheap, that's the way you are." Mama replies, "I'm proud to be cheap . . . I mean, y'all got clothes on your back, you have food in your belly, you got a place to live." Jessica replies, "I ain't got no food in my belly today! I ate nothin'!" And Mama says, "Don't worry, I think you can survive a little bit. Use the floatation devices."

Conversations in Regifting

ALANA: What's this?

MAMA JUNE: Cup holders.

ALANA: Can we give him this?

MAMA JUNE: I don't know, I think I might keep that one.

ALANA: What is that?

MAMA JUNE: A bookend.

ALANA: What's a bookend?

MAMA JUNE: A bookend is like when you hold . . . well . . . normally you have two bookends . . . it's like a, like a bookend. Something like that, it don't matter.

TIP #1: For shidness' sake, don't tell them it's a regift. It's from the heart. Although the presents are being regifted, like the hot sauce Alana received for her birthday, you should still choose carefully and try to pick something that the person getting the gift will like. And be sure to maintain plausible deniability. "I'm not gonna tell you it's been regifted," says June. "It come from the heart."

TIP #2: Regifting is a cycle. When you get a gift you don't want, save it so it can be regifted later. But just remember—the regift that you give might soon be regifted to someone else! As Uncle Poodle says when he gets his one bookend: "I'm gonna regift this next year. Somebody better look out 'cause they gonna get it next year." If a gift is still in circulation after a couple of years and everyone in the family has already received it, you can retire it by donating it to Goodwill or the Salvation Army. Another family might pick it up and the cycle of regifting will begin again.

TIP #3: The Ultimate Regift. This trick is difficult. To do it, you're going to need a good memory and nerves of steel. The goal is to receive a gift from a person and then to give it back to the same person without them even realizing that it is a regift. June says, "I think the ultimate regift to somebody would have to be wait a couple years, when they're not really thinking about the gift, and actually give it back to them. Or give it to them for their birthday! That's the ultimate thing.

I've done that **** too. Get something for Christmas, or get something for your birthday, and give it to them the next holiday. That's the ultimate."

Dumpster Dive!

The local department store, a.k.a. the Wilkinson County dump, is another place the family gets great deals—even better deals than at the flea market. If you really want to find some cheap gifts or household appliances redneck-style, then head to your local dump. You'd be amazed at the things you can find there with a little effort. Mama June is pretty excited when she finds almost-working speakers, and the rest of the family manages to find everything else—from mattresses to toilet seats to cribs. Just wipe everything down before you give it to family and friends!

Leftovers for Breakfast or Dinner!

This is the biggest redneck shortcut of them all. As we saw in chapter 3, "June in the Kitchen," Mama makes her multi-meals using mainly leftovers from her refrigerator. And the family makes sausage in the garage using roadkill (don't try this at home, folks!). A thrifty shortcut is to use absolutely everything you can from the refrigerator—in a multi-meal, in an omelet, stir-fried, or however else you can use it. Don't waste food, don't waste money—there are savings to be had everywhere!

Chapter 5

PUMPKIN'S PATCH

I'll stop passing gas when I'm dead.

—Pumpkin

As Alana says on the show's very first episode, Lauryn—a.k.a. Pumpkin—is "the craziest." A truer statement has never been made. If there is a food challenge, Pumpkin will take it on, whether it's pig's feet, pork chops, or the Pigzilla. Nicknamed for her favorite Halloween costume, Pumpkin has never been the same since she was hit by lightning. Her wacky antics—and even wackier statements—have made her a fan favorite and a big reason millions of people tune in each week. So here we'd like to present "Pumpkin's Patch"—ten of her wackiest quotes and the meanings behind them. Because it's impossible to choose which of her statements are the funniest, the quotes below are presented in no particular order. We just love us some Pumpkin!

The Ten Greatest Quotes of Miss Lauryn Shannon (a.k.a. Pumpkin)

1. "That's an awesome goal. That's the second thing beside my butthole piercing. That's the next thing."

On the first *Here Comes Honey Boo Boo* episode, Jessica talks about how she's been trying to lose weight and dress a little nicer because she's having trouble fitting in at school. She asks June a fateful question: "Will you lose weight with me if I lose weight?" June answers that she's happy with herself but will do it to support Jessica. At one point, June told her four daughters that if they fart twelve to fifteen times a day they can lose a lot of weight, so Jessica is hoping that this will help her in her quest. They begin the diet by each getting on the scale for a weigh-in to see their starting points—Jessica weighs 175 pounds, Pumpkin weighs 164, and Mama weighs 309. Jessica wants to lose 20 or 30 pounds and says she's going to begin dieting the very next day. However, she is soon caught walking around and stuffing packaged fat cakes into her pie hole. When Mama June goes out on her big eight-year-anniversary date with Sugar Bear, she tells him, "You can't tell Jessica I ate all this . . . 'cause I'm sure she's sneaking food in the house when I'm not there." When they gather again in a month or so to do another weigh-in, Jessica is at 172, so she has lost 3 pounds, and Mama ends up having lost 1.6 pounds. However, when Pumpkin gets on the scale, it turns out that she has gained 8 pounds and now weighs 172! Mama doesn't think that's very good and voices her disapproval, but Pumpkin assures her that her final goal is actually to weigh 250 pounds. "That's not a very good goal," Mama says, and Pumpkin replies, "That's an awesome goal. That's the second thing beside my butthole piercing. That's the next thing."

2. "My mama thinks I need etiquette classes. Look at me. I don't need no etiquette classes. I don't need manners or anything. What you see is what you get."

Mama June invites an etiquette coach over to give Alana some lessons in manners. She thinks this will give Alana an edge when she competes in the big pageants, because the judges at the Beautiful Faces of GA pageant told Alana that she needed to be more refined. Mama also thinks Pumpkin could really benefit from taking some etiquette lessons. As Mama says, out of all her kids, "Pumpkin needs to be more refined because she needs to be able to learn some manners." Pumpkin doesn't agree. In any case, the instructor arrives and starts to work with the girls, who don't seem the least bit interested. Both of them are staring into space. The instructor goes over the five ingredients of a first meeting: (1) stand for all introductions; (2) S-M-I-L-E; (3) make eye contact; (4) introduce yourself; and (5) shake hands. She points out that manners are all about kindness and having respect for people. Pumpkin replies, "I don't care what people think of me. I am what I am; if you don't like me, you don't like me," and the instructor drily replies, "I hope that works for you." After this lesson, they all move into the kitchen for some dining etiquette. The instructor puts place settings in front of them and shows them how to pick up a napkin from the top left side. As she is giving them the napkin demonstration, Pumpkin picks hers up and loudly blows her nose with it. Then Pumpkin asks the instructor if farting at the table is rude. ("The height of rudeness" is the reply.) At the end, the instructor points out that the girls have a long way to go and have a lot of habits they need to break. Alana sums the experience up by saying, "Etiquette classes are for stupid people." (In other words, just be yourself! It's stupid to try to be otherwise.) And Mama June, who admits that the instructor is a bit more square than her family is, says, "No one can be proper and etiquettely all the time. I don't care who you are."

3. "It was a good day because I saw my mama's forklift foot and it was so nasty."

Hard to believe, but the trip to Splash in the Boro water park is the very first time the family has ever seen June's mangled foot. She will just never take her socks off no matter what the situation is, and the girls had always been dying (dying!) of curiosity over what this foot might look like. After seeing a bunch of vajiggle-jaggle, going down the lazy river on blow-up inner tubes, and sliding down lots of slides (which were able to hold up Mama June nicely), the girls are finally able to witness the Foot. Mama June explains how she got the injury and that she's very protective of her feet—even Sugar

Bear isn't allowed to see it. But Mama, after years of badgering, grows weary of hearing the complaints and decides to show them just to make them happy. "Show it now!" screams Alana. When Mama June does take the sock off, Alana says, "That's disgusting!" Mama June tells Pumpkin that now that she's seen the forklift foot, it's time to go home. Mama and the girls pack everything up to leave the park. Pumpkin sums up the day by saying, "It was a good day because I saw my mama's forklift foot and it was so nasty."

Pumpkin's Real (Eye) Patch

Whether it's a snowball fight, a grass fight, a mud fight, a food fight, or dodgeball—it's only funny till somebody loses an eye. You've also got to watch out for keys. Just ask Pumpkin. One day, Sugar Bear tosses her the keys to his truck, with disastrous results. As Mama June says, "Pumpkin had a freak accident with a set of keys." Sugar Bear reports, "Pumpkin come to me and wanted keys to the truck. It was locked so I . . . do like I always do. I threw 'em to her. She missed 'em and they hit her in the face." The problem is that Sugar Bear's key ring is bigger than Glitzy! Unfortunately the accident leaves Pumpkin with a pretty serious injury. Pumpkin is rushed to the hospital for treatment and placed on strict bed rest to allow the eye to heal—which means no trick-or-treating! "Pumpkin is pretty bummed out that she's not going to be able to go trick-or-treating," says Mama June, "but Alana and her have talked and Alana's going to go trick-or-treating for her." Unfortunately for Pumpkin, the doctors discover that her eye injury is worse than originally thought and she has what is called a "detached retina." This is a medical emergency that requires immediate surgery. If it's not treated, you can go blind. Thankfully, Pumpkin is okay, although she is laid up on bed rest throughout most of Halloween and Thanksgiving, where she has to smack a pan with a metal spoon in order to get attention. So, if you're playing a game and someone whips an ice ball at your head, remember to think about what happened to Pumpkin. Make them stop by telling them what Mama June told her girls when they smacked her with a dodgeball: "I'm fixing to nut up on you now. You hit me in my face again, it's gonna be ugly out there."

4. "She lifted her leg and farted on my side."

The clan decides to mix it up one night and go out as a family to a barbecue joint for dinner. Mama cooks at home for the family every night, and Sugar Bear works seven days a week at his job, so this is a rare opportunity for them to all go out together. The barbecue place is decorated with pigs everywhere—just like Glitzy! "Oh my God, I see pigs everywhere!" says Alana. "We are pigs," says Sugar Bear. Soon they start looking over the menu options, and Alana says, "I want the barbecue. And then I want the chicken. And then I want the ribs." Alana decides she wants to order the barbecue and the chicken, along with ribs as her side dish. "Why can't my sides be meat?" she asks Mama. "Because, that's not how it works," Mama says. Mama ends up ordering the triple-meat combo with two sides, potato salad and baked beans, for Alana and tells the waitress that Alana's eyes are bigger than her stomach. The family digs in and eats up the delicious food. All of a sudden, Pumpkin says to Jessica, "I *know* you did not just fart on me. She lifted her leg and farted on my side." Mama June is mortified and tries to keep them quiet, but to no avail. This family loves a good fart joke.

5. "I like Halloween 'cause I like messing with people."

Halloween is one of the family's favorite holidays because they get to have fun and play pranks on people. And Pumpkin in particular likes messing

with people. When Halloween day arrives, Pumpkin gets up early and starts lurking under the house, looking for something. She emerges from a small door with a dirty, slimy piece of fabric, which she ties to a stick. Then she goes into Mama's bedroom while she's asleep and hangs the piece of fabric over her face, waking her up in a totally disgusting way. "What in the hell is that?!" says a half-asleep Mama June. Pumpkin gets a huge kick out of scaring Mama and waking her up. "I have no idea what it was on a stick

she had," Mama says. Then Pumpkin moves on to Jessica, Anna, and Alana, waking them all up with the nasty fabric. Happy Halloween, folks! Thankfully, Sugar Bear is spared, since he is recovering from a four-wheeler accident. The girls are very excited about Halloween because they're going to eat a lot of sweets. As Alana says, "Halloween is all about treats . . . treatin' myself to candy!"

6. "A baby does not come out of your butt!"

One day, when Anna is in her third trimester and due with baby Kaitlyn in about two weeks, the family is sitting around in the living room. Anna isn't feeling very well and is kind of mopey, and Mama says she's not sure Anna is ready to be a mommy yet. She still has a lot of growing up to do, in Mama June's opinion. Alana, for her part, is very excited about the impending delivery: "Kaitlyn's gonna come out of Anna's moon pie any day now!" Mama June asks Anna if she's feeling any better after the doctor's visit, and Anna says that she still has a lot of pressure in her butt area. Pumpkin helpfully advises, "A baby does not come out of your butt! It comes out of your biscuit." At this point, Mama June has the unfortunate job of informing the girls that a woman will sometimes poop the bed while she's in labor. "A woman will eww on herself before she has a baby. And then her hemorrhoids will come out." The girls are so grossed out and beg Mama June to "shut up!" Sugar Bear adds that if Anna does get hemorrhoids, Jessica will have to "pack 'em back in for her." And Alana says, "Anna started having contractions, and that's when you pull your baby out with your biscuit." Another successful science lesson for the Shannon/Thompson clan!

Pumpkin and Shugie

"I think that what attracted me to Sugar Bear is him and Pumpkin kind of had an instant connection," says Mama June. Sugar Bear and Mama June met in an online chat room. What was supposed to be a hook-'em-and-book-'em-type situation turned into nine years of unwedded bliss (plus one child). Although Sugar Bear isn't Pumpkin's biological father, that doesn't matter to Shugie. "I consider all the girls my daughters," he says. When Mama explains the situation, she says, "Sugar Bear is only Alana's biological daddy—" but Pumpkin interrupts her and says, "Is Pumpkin *and* Alana's biological daddy." The two of them have a bond that just can't be broken. As Pumpkin says, "I do consider Sugar Bear as a father figure. He might as well be my daddy."

7. "Marannaise does not have meat in it. You cannot be a vegetarian of marannaise."

Around Halloween, the girls decide they're going to help Mama get over her fear of mayonnaise. (See "Mayo-phobia" on page 59.) Alana pours (or glops) three large jars full of mayo into a bowl and places it in front of Mama June at the kitchen table. Mama is thoroughly disgusted by it and can't even look, but Jessica points out that this is stupid: "It's just mayonnaise," she says. "It's white and it's mayonnaise. It's like ketchup but it's white." Mama answers, "Okay, I don't see you eating it." And Jessica says, " 'Cause I'm a vegetarian." Mama June questions whether Jessica was ever a vegetarian, and Pumpkin exclaims, "You cannot be a vegetarian of marannaise . . . marannaise is something you put on a sammich!" Needless to say, when confronted with the bowl of mayo, Mama starts to have a full-on panic attack. As Alana says, "Mama was turning white . . . just like mayonnaise!"

Did Mama June really have a "panic ******* attack" when faced with all that gross mayonnaise? Everyone knows Mama June has a phobia about mayonnaise. When the kids confront her with an entire bowl of the stuff, Mama June has what a professional would call an adverse reaction. "My anxiety level is up like beyond the roof," she says. "I mean, like my chest is real tight. My throat feels like it's gonna close up." These are legitimate symptoms of a panic attack and Mama June's distress is probably quite real. One of the symptoms of a panic attack is an intense desire to escape, and sure enough, when Alana tries to smear some mayonnaise on Mama June, June loses it and flees: "Y'all gotta get that outta there, c'mon now, aa gaa aa bee, I'm gonna go into a full panic ******* attack igl giligl olgi uhh. Y'all gotta get it outta here *for real*!!"

A mayonnaise phobia is not currently recognized by professionals; there's no name for it. But that doesn't mean it's not a real thing. Ironically, being gradually exposed to the thing that you're irrationally afraid of is a real way to get over a phobia, but June would probably be better off seeking the help of a professional. Perhaps she can find a psychiatrist of marannaise.

8. "Mama, it removes your neck crust!"

Pumpkin says this awesome line during one of the family's trips to the supermarket. Mama June, of course, is going through her coupons and trying to figure out what she can use to get mad bargains. She's doing her "quick math" when Pumpkin runs over with some rust remover and says, "Look what I found! Mama, it removes your neck crust! Look. Read it." So, what exactly is that crust on Mama's neck? Some horrible disease? Or just some grime that got stuck in the cracks? Pumpkin says, "That crust on her neck. I don't know what it is. I guess she just don't scrub her neck when she's taking a bath." Mama explains that she's not letting herself go, she just looks good when she wants to look good. And her perfect answer to Pumpkin when she runs over with the rust remover? "You're stupid."

9. "Mama, no, we're not going on to that convo. No one gives a **** about your sex life."

It's the Christmas season, and Alana finally gives Sugar Bear the wig head she bought for him. "That's that nasty-ass head you bought at a flea market," Jessica says. Sugar Bear likes the gift a lot, pointing out that he does like to run his hands through Mama June's hair because "it's soft and smells good." After this, they have one more gift that needs to be opened. Turns out that Sugar Bear has a gift for Mama June, even though he says, "Whatever I bring in, you ain't never happy with." Anna points out, "You got her Alana, that's it, she loves that." And Mama June says, "That's about the only gift you ever gave me, was Smoochie, and I love it." Pumpkin helpfully offers, "It came out of your pa-doose. It didn't come out of his." Mama replies, "But it took two to tango." And Pumpkin says, "Mama, no, we're not going on to that convo. No one gives a **** about your sex life." When Mama finally does open the gift, it is . . . another damn deer statue! Mama June is a bit disappointed. Sugar Bear tries to be romantic, but Mama June says, "Deer are not romantic to me." Jessica calls her ungrateful, and poor Sugar Bear is sent outside to put the new deer statue present with the other one, out on the front steps.

10. "I believe that me getting struck by lightning has changed me forever, because I used to be really smart, and now I'm in between."

As Mama June explains, "About six or seven years ago, Pumpkin got struck by lightning when she was playing a game system." The old wives' tale is true: if lightning hits a power line it can travel down the line, into your house, into your game system, and then into you. So if there's thunder and lightning outside, put down the controller or you might get zapped! Mama says, "Pumpkin's never been the same since she got her brain fried." Alana helpfully draws before-and-after illustrations that show how Pumpkin has changed since this horrific event: Normal Pumpkin vs. Crazy Pumpkin and Uncooked Pumpkin vs. Cooked Pumpkin. As Alana says, "I love my sister, but she's been crazy ever since she got whopped by lightning." On *Here Comes Honey Boo Boo*, Pumpkin inspires this little ditty:

It's always something with Pumpkin!

Late one night, her brain was fried,
Now she's got a funny side.
It's always something with Pumpkin!
She's unique, it ain't disputed,
Since she got electrocuted.
It's always something with Pumpkin!

Doctors say that it's true that getting whopped by lightning can change your personality. Wouldn't you be cranky if you were zapped by millions of volts of electricity? Still, if you get struck by lightning, please be safe and consult a doctor.

Chapter 6

FUN AND GAMES

If you're not having fun and making memories,
then it's not worth the experience. We are who we are.
We like to have fun. If you're not having fun, then why
do it to begin with?

—Mama June

One thing the Shannon/Thompson family knows how to do is *have fun*, and during the course of *Here Comes Honey Boo Boo*, the family does everything from visiting the Redneck Games in East Dublin, Georgia, to getting manicures and s'mages at the local spa, to throwing a Christmas in July fund-raiser. Nothing is off-limits (or too messy) for this crew to try out. (Well, in retrospect maybe the indoor redneck waterslide was too messy, but that's not the point. The point is it was fun!) In this chapter, we'll go over all the fun and crazy things the family has done together, as well as some of their charity work during the holidays. As Mama likes to say, life is all about making memories with your kids and your family. So grab some butter and oil and your teacup pig and join the Shannon/Thompson crew as they get their fun on.

Yee-haw, Redneck Games!

The Redneck Games is an annual event in south Georgia, and it's all about Southern pride. As the official website says, it's "more fun than indoor plumbing." The games started in 1996 as a fun and wacky homage to the Summer Olympics in Atlanta, which many people had jokingly said was being hosted by rednecks. (Opening ceremony with silver pickup trucks, anyone?) The Redneck Games ended up being more popular and better attended than anyone ever expected, and they are still held annually to this day. Mama June points out, "It's a lot like the Olympics, but with a lot of missing teeth and a lot of butt cracks showing." Mama and Sugar Bear decide to take the kids to this event over the summer as a treat—woo-hoo! Pumpkin is planning on bobbing for pig's feet at the games. (While they may sound disgusting, pig's feet—also called "trotters"—are a Southern favorite and were once a delicacy in the United States.) Before the event, Pumpkin wants to practice the bobbing, and since Mama June doesn't have pig's feet lying around the house, they improvise with cold hot dogs (which Pumpkin and Alana both eat cold when she's finished practicing). When they get to the event, Mama is disgusted to see that the pig's feet are raw and there's no "cookedness" to them at all. Pumpkin gives it her best shot but ends up losing after getting only two pig's feet: "I just competed in the pig's feet thing and I got two pig's feet," she says. "Did my family proud, though." Sugar Bear had a slightly different take on it: "Pumpkin bobbing for pig's feet at the Redneck Games. Pbbt. She bombed out."

Later on, the girls want to go swimming in a nearby body of water, but Mama June is too worried about them catching a certain flesh-eating bacteria that's been rumored to be in those waters. So, instead, Alana and crew head over to the mud belly flop to give that a try. This involves standing at the edge of a pit and then jumping straight into the mud. Pumpkin, Jessica, and Alana all have an amazin' time flopping belly-first right into the mud. "I just did the mud belly flop and I did awesome. Hit my belly, my belly's kinda burnin'," says Jessica. Alana is a little scared at first but then can barely be dragged out of that pit, saying, "I like to get dirty like a pig!" Although they didn't win, Alana was proud of her accomplishment: "I just did a belly flop and I did awesome and I'm the best and I'm gonna flop again." Mud belly flops are a redneckificent activity for the entire family—and also very good for the skin. All in all, a wonderful time was had by everyone at the Redneck Games. As Mama June puts it, "We came. We conquered. We done what needed to be done. We kicked a little bit of redneck tail today. And wow. Peace. Deuces." If you're interested in eating raw trotters, getting dirty in the mud, or trying to kick some redneck tail yourself, visit the games' website at SummerRedneck Games.com for the latest information.

TIP! If you have to use the bathroom, try to use the Port-a-Potty as early as possible, or "you're gonna be going into some filth."

Want to try bobbing at home? If you really want to do it with pig's feet, you can ask for them at your local butcher (where they sometimes keep them frozen) or even purchase them on Amazon. However, the majority of people will want to try hot dogs or plain ol' apples for this old-fashioned game. Get yourself a large tub, fill it with water, and add hot dogs or apples. If you'd like, you can set a time limit and see how many items each player can collect in that period (hopefully more than Pumpkin's two pig's feet!). Each person clasps her hands behind her back and then takes a turn trying to catch as many hot dogs or apples as possible with her teeth. If you have long hair, remember to tie it back, or you're going to have a face full of wet hair. And you'll have better luck if you try to pin the apple on the bottom of the tub rather than pluck it off the surface. Adults and children alike will have a hilarious time getting soaked as they try to gather more than anybody else! Because who doesn't like cold hot dogs?

Mani-Pedis June-Style

Nothing says "redneck" like great personal grooming—so when the local salon is running a weekly special that Mama June can't pass up, she decides to treat the girls to manicures and pedicures. She and Alana also plan on getting facials—Alana wants her skin soft for an upcoming pageant, and Mama June wants to look nice for her eight-year-anniversary date with Sugar Bear. Because before you put some new paint on the barn, sometimes you need to get the barn power washed and maybe apply a decent coat of primer. Mama June loves the facial and thinks it's worth every penny, and Alana agrees, saying, "That facial felt so good, it felt like I had a baby's bottom on my cheeks." It's true—try it yourself! Next up—Pumpkin, Jessica, and Anna sit down to get pedicures. They've never had pedicures before and their feet are a "hot mess," according to Mama June. The Bamm-Bamm look has its downside, so it's up to the manicurists to reverse the damage that's accumulated from years of walking to the convenience store with no shoes on. Jessica in particular has feet that are in pretty bad shape: "Her crusts on her feet can sandpaper the floor!" yells Anna. Luckily, manicurists are trained professionals with nerves of steel. When it comes to be Mama's turn, she refuses to take her socks off to get a pedicure because of her forklift foot. Pumpkin begs her— "Please, just do it for me, if you love me, you'll do it for me!" But at the end of the day, June just can't bring herself to take her socks off. Instead, the manicurist paints pretty pink toenails right on top of her socks where her toenails would be. (Even trained professionals have their limits.) At the end of the afternoon, the manicurist sums it up by saying, "It was an experience . . . I think I need to go home now."

While the Shannon/Thompson clan used couponing to finance their spa day, you can easily have a mani-pedi day at home for a fraction of the cost. Here are a few tips for a fun spa day on the cheap:

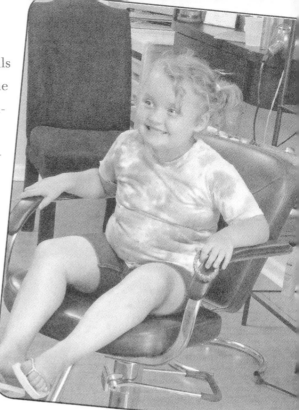

TIP #1: Just as the Shannon/Thompson girls did, make the day into an exciting adventure. Invite some friends or family members over so you can do each other's nails. If it's a nice day, everyone can sit outside on chairs—and that way, you won't have to clean up the mess in your house. Pick out some nice open-toed shoes, or just go with the Bamm-Bamm look to show off your soon-to-be-beautimous feet.

TIP #2: Be sure to stock up on a variety of nail polish colors and lots of cotton balls, polish remover, and emery boards. If you're feeling ambitious and want a real spa effect, you can also apply homemade or store-bought facial masks to each other (have cucumber slices available for people's eyes). Put some cold drinks in a cooler, put out some raw hot dogs and trotters and pretzels and cheese balls, and get ready for a lot of laughs (and a little salmonella).

TIP #3: Start your manicure with clean, dry nails. Really get under there and get out any gunk from when you were processing Logan. For a classic look, file nails short in a square shape with rounded corners. Not only does this look attractive, but it's an easier shape to paint at home and you won't break a nail when you're removing hog jowl. Be sure to take your socks off before you start applying the nail polish, unless you're hiding a forklift foot.

TIP #4: Choose the perfect color. You can either pick a flattering one that complements your skin tone or go crazy and pick a neon bright one that's fun and uplifting (and will help the rescuers find your body after the inevitable mud boggin' accident). Go nuts and paint every other nail a different color. Or just use whatever color was free—*free!*—with the use of your double-stacked coupon. It'll look better because you know it's free.

TIP #5: Be sure to apply a base coat first, and then apply two thin coats of polish. Finish with a top coat. To dry, grab some household fans and hold wet nails in front of them (a redneck nail dryer!).

TIP #6: If you do suffer from a terrible case of forklift foot and are too embarrassed to show your feet, just pick your colors and then paint them right over your socks, where your toes should be. Win-win for everybody.

Say Cheese, Y'all!

Taking a family photo is a classic, traditional activity that will leave you with a great memento to hang on your wall (or hide in your closet). Just be prepared to twist some arms to get all the family members involved. Mama June never had a family photograph taken but has always wanted one, so she and the family head to Milledgeville to a pretty location called the Boat Landing to meet up with a local photographer. Since this is summertime in Georgia, it's an incredibly hot day—and Anna is pregnant with baby Kaitlyn on top of that! The family decides to take the photo near the rocks, although it ends up being just the girls, because Mama doesn't want to climb all the way down: "Now, y'all know once y'all get down there y'all gonna have to come back up." Everyone's hot and irritated, and the clan looks a bit sweaty and shell-shocked in the final photographs. Plus, Alana's butt gets very dirty from sittin' on the rocks. As Mama June says, "Alana, no matter how dressy she is, she always seems to find the mud somewhere." The girls also have multiple arguments while trying to walk along the path holding hands—they can't stop bickering about how fast to walk and how exactly to grasp each other's hands. "In our family, if we're not yellin' at one another, something's gotta be wrong," says Mama June. Finally, the whole group gets in together for a photo and they all look beautimous, although Sugar Bear only has on pants and a T-shirt. That's okay with Mama though, because Sugar Bear is who he is. As he says himself, "I'm not the dress-up type. Unless it's a funeral." All in all, it's a great experience for the family to get a photograph taken, but Alana sums things up by saying, "It was so hot and everybody was so mopey."

A family photograph can be a very fun (and bonding) daytime activity to do with the entire family. If you've never had one done before (as in Mama June's case), it can be fascinating for the kids to see how the process works, and at the end of the day, your family will have a treasured keepsake to display. If you decide to have a family portrait of your own taken, here are a few tips that will make the process go as smoothly as possible.

TIP #1: Find your photographer soul mate! Be sure you have a photographer you are comfortable with. Whether it's a family friend who's interested in photography, somebody you have a coupon for, or just the person at the local photography studio, make sure you meet them and talk to them first so that the entire family feels comfortable. When you feel at ease with the photographer, it makes the entire process go more smoothly and can even help get the big smiles you need for this treasured family moment. Also, if this is an established photographer, you might want the entire family to look at his or her portfolio or blog online (if available) to make sure everyone is happy with the choice.

TIP #2: Pick the perfect spot! As we've learned from the Shannon/Thompson clan, it's important to choose just the right place in the right weather. Think about where the photograph will go in your house and how you'd like it to look. Do you want water behind your group, or a field with trees, or a beach? Or do you want the photo to be taken at home? Pick whatever scene is meaningful to you and your family and will mesh well with the environment where the photo will be displayed.

Once you have the scene chosen, try to find a time when that particular scene will look best and the family will be most comfortable. A comfortable family will make a great-looking photograph! An in-store studio is also a good choice when taking a family photograph, and in that case, you don't have to worry about the weather going haywire.

TIP #3: Think of this as a natural pageant! It's good to look nice for the family photograph, but don't feel the need to get too glammed up (or sassified, for that matter). This is especially true in 100-degree weather, 'cause you'll end up looking like a linebacker with mascara running down your cheeks if you wear too much makeup. A natural look is just fine and is how you picture your family anyway. As Mama June says, "Beauty comes within. I mean, if you've got a great personality and everything . . . it shines through on the outside." Don't worry about having the entire family in matching outfits, unless that's what you want. That look can certainly be nice and be fun, but an individual look for each person that complements the whole can be even better. Just be certain that the outfits don't clash with each other! You'll regret having to look at that hot mess every day of your life.

TIP #4: Rest up and be organized! Make sure the entire family is well rested and prepared in advance of the big day. If you have kids, you know them and which time of the day they're at their best. You know exactly how much rest they need before taking part in an activity, so plan ahead and make sure everyone gets the optimal amount. Organize everything in advance—clothing, props, transport, payment, etc. The more comfortable, well rested, and organized the family is, the better the experience will be for everyone involved.

TIP #5: Say excuse me! Hold all burps and farts in until the photograph is finished. Or, if you really have to let loose, wait until the photographer says "cheese" and then let it rip. That will be quite the family photograph and one that's taken the Honey Boo Boo way!

TIP #6: If you don't ever succeed in getting the perfect shot, there's always Photoshop. If you don't have access to a computer, you can combine several photos using scissors and glue—a.k.a. redneck Photoshop!

Splish Splash—and Hide That Vajiggle-jaggle!

As a reward for losing at least a little bit of weight on the diet challenge (okay, some of them gained weight, but who's counting?), Mama decides to take the girls to the Splash in the Boro water park for the day. The girls are very excited, since this is their first time ever at a water park. Alana dons a yellow life jacket and observes, "This life jacket makes me look like a chunky lemon." First up is the lazy river, where the girls and their mama just float along in inner tubes. Pumpkin notes, "A good activity for the fat folk is just the lazy river." The girls also go down lots of slides and play in water-soaked playgrounds with sprinklers. They even get to see their mama go down the slide. But what do the girls enjoy the most about this day? Finally getting to see Mama's forklift foot. Some things money just can't buy! For a fun outing with your family on a steaming-hot day, look into visiting your local water park. If funds are tight or you simply can't get to a water park, there's nothin' better than homemade—check out "Build a Redneck Waterslide" on page 38.

TIP! Choose your swimwear carefully. Make sure it fits properly and that it's a bright color so your family can find you easily. And make sure it hides that vajiggle-jaggle.

Happy Birthday to Yooooouuuuuu!

When Alana's seventh birthday comes up, the family decides to have a big party. On the morning of, Anna, Pumpkin, and Jessica get together to decide what to give Alana for her birthday. None of them have any money (Anna says, "All I have is this piece of tape") and not one of them feels like they are creative enough to make something. So they decide to go into Mama June's stockpile of staples and take some items that she has acquired with her couponing. They grab soap, Pop-Tarts, and a huge industrial-size bottle of hot sauce. Together, they wrap the "presents" and put so much tape around each one that Alana will never be able to open them. Then the big party gets set up on the lawn—woo-hoo! At the party they have a pool, a big blow-up waterslide, drinks, a snow cone machine, and lots of food—including hot dogs that are even cooked. "Happy birthday to me!" says Alana. The big waterslide is a huge success and even Mama June tries to climb up it, with the entire party chanting, "June, June, June!" Unfortunately, "forklift foot and gravity" keep her from climbing up, but at least she tried. After the food and fun, Alana thanks everyone for coming and opens up her presents. Her favorite presents, of course, are the soap and hot sauce from her sisters, because "they came from the heart." At the end of the day, Alana proclaims this the best birthday ever.

TIP! A seven-year-old is probably the only person who would think hot sauce comes from the heart. But that's okay, we won't tell. When you're stockpiling your unwanted presents to regift later, try to have some that are appropriate for all ages.

Go-Karting

Speaking of birthdays, when it's time for Sugar Bear's forty-first birthday, the family throws him a *Dukes of Hazzard*–themed birthday party. *The Dukes of Hazzard* is Sugar Bear's favorite show, and Daisy Duke is his favorite character. Alana has the great idea to ask a family friend to make a Daisy Duke piñata for Sugar Bear's birthday, shaped like her favorite short-shorts. But then Alana has the even *better* idea for the family to take Shugie go-karting for his birthday. A go-kart is a small, four-wheeled vehicle that you race on a track. Lots of amusement parks have go-kart tracks, but there are also places you can go specifically for go-karting. The family heads to Adventure Crossing in Augusta,

Georgia, for some go-karting action. Right away, the girls try to convince Mama to go riding with them ("Mama, you need to ride with us!"), but she refuses. Since Mama is legally blind, she absolutely will not drive anything. The girls and Shugie have a fantastic time racing each other around the track, while Mama stays on the sidelines with baby Kaitlyn, screaming, "Jessica! Put the gas to it!" Pumpkin says, "The best go-kart rider . . . that was me." Finally, the girls nag Mama June so much that she gives in and decides to ride just so she can shut them up. "How do you even drive? I don't know where the gas thing is!" says Mama June. After she settles into a kart—Alana says, "I'm really proud of my mama for getting in that go-kart"—Mama June takes off. The girls chastise Mama for driving too slow, but she explains that her eyesight is a bit blurry, so she "just kinda like followed the course." At one point, two young men have to help Mama by pushing her go-kart. As Mama explains, "When I got stuck two guys had to actually, like, push me from behind. And they were laughing because, ya know, I am big and voluptuous, so it took two. But I think maybe, wait, there was three." Aside from the assist from the two/three boys and the two times Jessica runs into her, Mama June does pretty good on the track. When she pulls her kart up, she has a bit of trouble getting out. But then Mama says, "It was actually pretty cool ridin' 'em. I actually had a lot of fun." Much like Alana did, Sugar Bear sums up the experience by saying, "This was my best birthday ever."

Troup's Farm for Pumpkins

When Halloween time comes around the family is very excited. As Mama says, "Halloween's a big thing for the girls 'cause they like dressing up and eating a lot of candy." They all decide to take a trip to a pumpkin patch so they can pick out their own pumpkins to carve. The family heads to TroupCorn, a.k.a. Troup's Farm, which Mama describes as "a redneck pumpkin patch—you're just out in the middle of someone's property." To get to the pumpkins, you can either take a hayride or ride the cows, which are cow-painted barrels on wheels that are pulled along by a pickup truck. The girls, of course, decide to take the cows and have a crazy ride. Then each person starts hunting for his or her pumpkin. The girls all pick out pumpkins for themselves, and they pick out the biggest, most wopsided one in the patch for Mama because it looks just like her and "her big head." ("Mama's big," says Alana.) Mama explains that she is not wopsided, she's just "curviness" and "beautimous." After loading up their pumpkins, the girls play ball in the hayfield, but it quickly turns into a game of "hit Mama in the face with a ball." Back at the house, Uncle Poodle comes over with his own pumpkin to join the family in some pumpkin-carving fun. The family starts carving, and they soon begin having tons of fun playing with the goopy insides. As Sugar Bear says, "As soon as I realized that the insides were such a gooey mess, I knew we were in trouble." The girls and Uncle Poodle get into a huge pumpkin fight, smearing the pumpkin insides down each other's pants, in each other's hair—even all over the baby. At the end of the day, everyone has a nicely carved pumpkin—except Poodle, who puts his head inside Mama June's pumpkin and can't get it out. The whole family tries to help him, with no success, so they all go back inside the house while Poodle sits on the porch with his new pumpkin head (and Mama almost pees herself because she can't stop laughing).

Pumpkin carving is a great, inexpensive activity that the whole family can do together. And nothing quite says Halloween like the sight of a glowing jack-o'-lantern on your front lawn or steps. Besides, just look at all the laughs the Shannon/Thompson clan has when they give it a try! If you've never carved pumpkins and you want to try this at home, here are some homegrown tips for you and your family:

Tip #1: How big? Think about what size pumpkin you'd like to have, and then find one with few to no bruises or blemishes so the end result looks as pretty as possible. Do you want small pumpkins for your windowsill or a huge one for your front steps? Make sure yours isn't wopsided like Mama June's, because you want the pumpkin to be able to stand up straight and not flop over.

Tip #2: Get your tools ready. Wipe down your pumpkin of choice with a wet paper towel, and spread out some sheets of newspaper to work on top of. Set up a bowl next to you for the pumpkin guts. Be sure to have a pencil, a long knife, a large metal spoon, and a smaller knife for detail work on hand. You will also need a candle to place inside the jack-o'-lantern when you're finished. Use the pencil to draw a face or design on the pumpkin or pumpkins that you want to carve. If you're stumped for ideas, you can also purchase stencils or a pumpkin-carving kit from craft stores, Halloween stores, or places like Target and Walmart.

Tip #3: Start carving! As they did on *Here Comes Honey Boo Boo,* use a big knife to cut a circle in the top of the pumpkin (around the stem) and aim the tip of the knife toward the center for an angled cut. (Don't cut the bottom of the pumpkin by mistake, like Mama June does.) Use a big spoon to scoop out the guts of the pumpkin, or be like Sugar Bear and just use your hands. Be careful—this is the time when a pumpkin fight is most likely to break out. Don't let anyone shove pumpkin seeds down your pants.

Tip #4: Final details. Scrape the inside of the pumpkin clean, and then use the small knife to cut the pumpkin along the lines you sketched out. When you're finished carving everything, smooth over any rough or jagged pieces with the small knife.

Tip #5: Display! Find a spot for your pumpkin and place your choice of candle inside. Light the candle with a long kitchen match so you don't burn yourself. If you've destroyed the pumpkins while having a pumpkin fight, leave the pieces out on the lawn for the deer to eat. Enjoy your handiwork while eating lots of candy! (As Alana says, "Halloween is all about treats . . . treating myself to candy!")

Kackleberry Farm Corn Maze

The family decides to head to Kackleberry Farm in Georgia for some Halloween-time fun, including the corn maze, zip line, and trampoline. Jessica says she'd like to rename the place "Cankleberry Farms," because her mom has cankles, which Jessica describes as "overlapped meat and can't see your ankles." After taking some photos with their heads in country fair cutouts, the family decides to head over to the corn maze. ("What's a corn maze?" asks Alana, and her mom answers, "A corn maze is where they grow, like, corn and they make it to be like . . . like a . . . like a . . . corn maze.") They have a great time exploring the maze, until Mama June realizes they've been walking around in circles for what seems like hours. Finally, Mama June has to pee and can't hold it any longer. She goes right into the corn and does her business; since she doesn't have anything to wipe herself with, she dries the old-fashioned way, with a "drip and dry" and a "little shake." "Mama had to drip dry!" says Alana. ("She watered it," says Sugar Bear.)

Finally, the family finds their way out of the maze, thanks to the ah-maze-ing Alana, who smells the ending and knows exactly which way to go. Before leaving, the family hits the trampoline and the zip line to round out a truly amazing fall day.

Sooo . . . what actually is a corn maze? A corn maze is, quite simply, a maze cut into a field of corn. In England, corn mazes are called maize mazes. Amazing! But what's a maze? Well, that's a puzzle you have to find the correct pathway to walk through. A good trick to remember when trying to solve a corn maze is to get oriented before you go inside: take note of which side the sun is on, or find a tower or a tall tree and remember where it is. You can also try the right-hand rule: stick out your right hand at the start of the maze and always have that hand touching a wall. Eventually you'll find your way out, as long as there are no tunnels or overpasses. Or you could try Alana's method and use your snooter: "C'mon, everybody, I smell the ending!" Hopefully you're not smelling whatever Mama June left as a special gift in the middle of the maze.

Halloween Tips, Honey Boo Boo-Style

Halloween is about more than sticking your head in jack-o'-lanterns, peeing in corn mazes, and scaring people with garbage on a stick. When you've perfected your Crap Paper Monster costume and the big night arrives, it's all about the trick-or-treating. In other words: CANDY! With a little work you can minimize your effort and maximize your haul. Here are a few tricks that will help you get the most treats—you might even have enough candy left over to give some to the grown-ups.

TIP #1: Scout out the best neighborhoods beforehand. Not everyone gives out candy on Halloween, so look for houses that have the lights on and decorations up. Mama June says, "We always go trick-or-treating at the Milledgeville Country Club. And I go around to, like, the different neighborhoods. 'Cause that's where the best candy is. Hello. That's where all the rich folks live." Some communities will have an event in town where you can trick-or-treat at local stores or country clubs or even take a hayride like the Shannon/Thompson kids do.

TIP #2: If you can't go, pick the right helper to get your candy for you. When Pumpkin is stuck in bed with an eye injury, she says, "I'm not gonna be able to go trick-or-treating this year, so I'm gettin' Alana to get my candy. And Alana's more aggressive so she'll grab a lot of candy." Picking the right accomplice can make the difference between getting the big candies and getting dental floss. The person you send has to be young and cute and appear honest so that people really will believe she's getting the candy for "her sick sister with a detached retina." Listen to Alana: "I get the most candy because I work it."

TIP #3: Check the candy. It's important to let the grown-ups check your candy before you eat it to make sure there are no unpleasant surprises . . . like fruits or vegetables. Or dental floss. Jessica says, "When I get fruits and vegetables, I think they're calling me fat." But Mama June is always there with some motherly advice: "When you get fruits and vegetables you pretty much throw them away. Be nice. Take 'em. And then throw them down once we get back to the trailer away from the house." When they get home June indeed does find a whole bunch of apples mixed in with the candy, so she gives them to Alana to throw out in the yard to "feed the deer."

TIP #4: Keep your eyes on the candy tester. Mama June starts testing the candy while the family is still out trick-or-treating. Jessica: "Mama, stop eating them!" Mama June: "Look, I gotta inspect the candy as we're trick-or-treatin'." If anyone offers to inspect your candy while you're trick-or-treating, be careful! It's a total scam. They are trying to steal your candy. All inspections should be done at home at the table. Even then, you've got to be vigilant. Alana says, "Mama, you too busy eatin' to check it." "That's the way to check it," Mama June says. "You gotta check a couple of pieces. I'm y'all's guinea pig."

Tɪᴘ #5: When it's your turn to dish out treats to happy Halloweeners—don't give out dental floss! As Alana says, "Who gives dental floss for Halloween? Some people are just plain crazy."

Ice Days at Olde Town Conyers Pavilion

To get the girls in the Christmas spirit (and to get them out of the dang house), June and Sugar Bear decide to take them ice-skating at Olde Town Conyers Pavilion. Alana gets out her warmest clothes since "she's gonna have to bundle her butt good to stay warm." The kids are very excited but also obstamistical, because they are worried about hurting themselves. Naturally, Alana, Pumpkin, and Anna slip and slide all over the place—but eventually Alana dubs herself "most improved." The family has a really great time on the ice, although it's rough going at first. Mama even gets herself smacked right in the face with a snowball (luckily she doesn't suffer a detached retina like Pumpkin did). Are you interested in getting your family in the Christmas spirit? Do they have cabin fever during such cold weather? Ice-skating is a great activity, but if your kids are a bit too, um, *apprehensum* about trying that, below are a few more winter activities you can do together as a family. Please note that it may be hard to pull these off in McIntyre, Georgia, but folks in many other parts of the country are free to try them out!

- Go sledding. This is a great activity to do together right after a snowfall. Not only is it exhilarating and tons of fun, it's great exercise. As long as you have an appropriate hill nearby (which most towns or cities do), all you need is a sled and some warm clothing. There are many different types of sleds you can use. Some people like to use a saucer sled (shaped like a circle); some like to use an old-fashioned flexible flyer; and some like to use a foam slider, which generally has handles and a smooth underside. All of these and more will work if you have a good sledding hill. If you really want to do this redneck-style, just find a flat piece of cardboard or the top of a garbage can and fly down that way! The best day for sledding is day two after it snows. On the first day, the snow is often too thick; on the third day, it's too slippery and icy. Day two is perfection!

- Build a snowman or a lot of snowmen. Building a snowman is a great family-bonding activity. Best of all, it can be done right on your front lawn, and you'll have an instant winter decoration. Lots of places sell snowman-making kits, which include fake eyes of coal, a fake carrot, a corncob pipe, and a scarf. You can certainly make a classic snowman and it will look great. However, if you want to be feugel, you can easily (and cheaply) customize your snowmen much like the family did when they made the Junecrow scarecrow. Just gather some clothes and other accessories from each member of your family from inside your house. Make as many snowmen as there are members of your family, and size them appropriately. Dress them up like each member, and soon your lawn will be decorated by these icy doppelgängers.

- Snowball fight! The most redneck wintertime activity of all. The Shannon/Thompson family has had more fights than you can count—grass fights, food fights, pumpkin-guts fights . . . you name it! Why not a snowball fight? This activity costs no money at all and can be done on its own, or you can tack it on the end of one of the above activities. Just remember—no head shots. It's only funny until somebody gets hit in the eye. And then gets a detached retina.

Christmas in July

In the middle of the summer, the family decides to hold "Christmas in July." Mama June and the crew set up huge Christmas decorations and lights on the lawn and try to take up donations to help some of the local charities. Of course, since this is Georgia, it's 100-plus degrees outside while they are trying to do this, which makes it very hard to get the family to help out with the setup—especially a very pregnant Anna and a naturally lazy Pumpkin. Mama June makes them keep workin' though, because she feels very strongly about helping people in need. Needless to say, it's no trouble getting Alana involved. She loves setting up the decorations and then running outside on the lawn with everything set up. Alana says, "When the decorations are up, it's real easy to know which house is yours." She feels as if all the blow-up figures, especially the Santa Clauses, are her friends and family. Once Sugar Bear, a.k.a. Shorty Claus, is able to get his costume on (in which he smells like a "chain-smoking goat"), he heads out to sit in the chair of honor. Despite having to wear that costume in such intense heat, Sugar Bear is happy because he enjoys giving back to the community. As child after child comes to sit on his lap—

asking for things like iPhones and four-wheelers—Sugar Bear gets into the spirit of Christmas. (Albeit in July.) Honey Boo Boo herself gets on his lap and asks for an iPhone, and they talk about Elvis, the toy-making Christmas elf. Shorty Claus tells her, "Be good for Mommy and Daddy, and we'll bring you some surprises this Christmas!" At the very end of the day, after all the kids are gone, Mama June finally gets a chance to sit on Santa's lap herself. As Sugar Bear points out, "she didn't really ask for nothin', but I couldn't feel my feet." The Christmas in July event was a rousing success for the Shannon/Thompson family and they collected a lot of donations. But they collect even *more* donations for charity when Christmastime actually rolls around . . .

Holladays Redneck-Style

When December comes and it's really time for Christmas, the Shannon/Thompson clan starts preparing for another Christmas charity drive so they can help those in need. Sugar Bear is even dusting off the ol' Shorty Claus costume! This is a huge deal for the family, as Christmas in July was, and they all pitch in while hanging hundreds of decorations on the front lawn. Mama June says, "We eat, breathe, and sleep the Christmas display for a month. There's nothing like this in our county." Sugar Bear works for several days putting decorations up, and Alana thinks if they get it done, it will be a Christmas miracle. Since this is going to be one of the family's biggest productions yet, some of the local neighbors come by to help set up the elaborate Christmas scene. Mama doesn't want to waste any of the decorations—when one tree decoration is clearly broken, Mama insists, "I can fix it! We ain't got money to waste to buy new." Alana says, "Mama is bat-poop crazy about Christmas decorations." After the front lawn is set up, Sugar Bear puts the (fake) family tree up in their living room. The girls all gather around to decorate it, but they can't seem to find a tree topper. Alana has the brilliant idea to put the family's new pet, Nugget the chicken, on top of the tree as the topper. Jessica picks up Alana (who is holding Nugget) and lifts her up so she can do the honors—but then the entire tree comes down! As Mama reasons, "It is what it is . . . you let kids decorate your tree, you're bound to have some kind of disaster happen." Hopefully Nugget is not too traumatized.

Honey Boo Boo's oversize Christmas decorations in the front yard are a family tradition that started with Sugar Bear's late mom, Nana, who passed away in 2009. Nana won the award for the best Christmas display in Wilkinson County for four years in a row, and Mama June continued the legacy for three years after that. It's a fun family tradition, but it's a lot of work and the whole family has to pitch in. "Yeah, it actually looks like Christmas threw up in our front yard," Mama June says. "It's somethin' to take very good pride in." When you're ready to beautify your own home for the holidays, here are some fun tips to help you make it look like Christmas threw up in *your* front yard.

TIP #1: Go big! You should have so many Christmas lights up that you can see the display from space. "Our house looks awesome," says Alana. "I'm pretty sure you can see our house from the moon." June says they put up around 100,000 lights a year, with twenty blow-ups and thirty to forty blow molds ("blow-ups" are the big inflatable Santa Claus and reindeer decorations and "blow molds" are the plastic displays of Jesus or snowmen that have lights inside them). Wrap lights around your bushes and trees "just like toilet paper." Add new stuff every year and keep changing up your layout so it's always exciting and different. "The bigger the better," Mama June says, and it's hard to argue with the results.

TIP #2: Never throw anything away! If you're going to accumulate hundreds of decorations for the ultimate display, you're going to have to be thrifty and repair and recycle your old trees and lights. "This is going in the trash this year, ain't it?" asks Sugar Bear as he takes a silver tree down from the storage space above the garage. "It still lights up!" answers Mama June. "It's your mother's!" The same thing happens when Pumpkin tries to throw away a broken tree display. "Let me see it!" yells Mama June. "I can fix it!" And you know what? Ta-dow! Mama June does fix it. Even if your decoration looks a little gimpy in the daylight, when it's dark outside nobody will be able to see that Baby Jesus's toe is all bit up. Remember Mama June's words: "As long as it lights up, it works, it's good."

TIP #3: Get the family and the neighbors involved! When you're setting up hundreds of lights and dozens of blow-ups, you're going to need help. Your family is a great source of cheap labor—they'll work for cheese balls and pig's feet! And it could even be a bonding experience; Mama June says that even though the family may complain and fight every year while they "bust their asses off" to set up the Christmas display, at the end of the day they really enjoy the time together and enjoy knowing it would make Nana happy. And when your insane Christmas display is done in the name of charity, you might even be able to get your neighbors to pitch in. Even the Grinchiest neighbor will have their heart grow three sizes when they're working for a good cause. And bonus: they won't be able to complain because they helped set it up!

When the day finally arrives for the big Christmas charity drive, the family is very excited. Mama June explains that helping people in her community is very important to her because when she was in need, somebody helped her out, so she wants to be able to help out the next person. June was that person at one time and didn't have Christmas for her kids. As she says, "It's not a fun experience for a parent to wake up to your child having nothing at Christmastime." June doesn't want anybody else to have to go through that, and that's why her family is committed to making these drives happen. Last Christmas, they were able to help 108 families, but their goal this year is to raise $10,000 or more in donations for needy families. When the sun goes down, the family lights up all the decorations and they stand outside, greeting the hundreds of people who come to the house to donate toys and cans of food. Alana puts on her Elvis outfit and stands next to Santa Claus, a.k.a. Shorty Claus. (This makes sense because Elvis is Santa's helper!) As Shorty begins to greet people, Pumpkin starts giving groups of people redneck tours of the yard, telling them many fun details, such as how long it took to put everything up and who broke what. At the end of the charity drive, the family ends up not only meeting but also exceeding all of their goals and expectations for the event. They raise more than $15,000 in cash and toys for needy families in the area!

The next day, they load all the donations onto a truck and drive them over to Miss Wanda, who runs one of the local charities, Wilco Luvs Kids. Miss Wanda was one of the people who helped June when she and her family were in need, and that opened June's eyes to wanting to help others in her community. As Wanda says, Mama June "has a big heart, and this year the family has really came through for me . . . the North Pole doesn't have this many toys." The family is very happy to have been able to help so many kids this year, and their goal is to do even more for their community in the future.

If you and your family would like to help out with donations during the holidays, there are lots of local churches, shelters, food banks, schools, and other organizations that would be happy to have your involvement. Look online or ask the people in your neighborhood to help you locate a place in your town. If you'd like to help on a national level, here are a few great charities that you can become involved with:

Great Charities

Make-A-Wish Foundation
Grants the wishes of children with life-threatening diseases.
www.wish.org

Toys for Tots
Raises funds to provide toys to supplement the collections of local coordinators and defray the costs of conducting annual Toys for Tots campaigns.
www.toysfortots.org

My Two Front Teeth
Their online wish tree lets you give toys, presents, and wishes to disadvantaged kids and needy children for Christmas and the holidays.
www.mytwofrontteeth.org

St. Jude Children's Research Hospital
An internationally recognized hospital known for its pioneering work in finding cures for and saving children with pediatric cancers.
www.stjude.org

Red Cross
Provides disaster relief at home and abroad, CPR certification and first aid courses, blood donation, and emergency preparedness.
www.redcross.org

The United Way
Envisions a world where all individuals and families achieve their human potential through education, income stability, and healthy lives.
www.unitedway.org

United Federation of Teachers Anti-Bullying Campaign
The UFT's BRAVE campaign aims to combat bullying in our schools.
www.uft.org/our-rights/brave

Redneckulous Romance, Part II

When Mama June dyes her hair blond, it inspires Shugie to get creative in the romance department. "Her new blond hair gave me a great idea so I ordered a costume for June." A smexy, revealing costume. Mama June sashays out dressed as a blond bombshell (Hubba Bubba!) and Sugar Bear is instantly smitten: "When June came out as Marilyn Monroe I instantly became Horny Bear." But the kids are less than impressed. "What the hell is wrong with your tan?" asks Jessica. "She looked like Napoleon ice cream," Anna says. "Some part was pink, some part was chocolate, some part was vanilla, and it looked just raunchy. I don't want to eat that ice cream."

However, there was a certain bear who was interested in that particular flavor of ice cream:

HORNY BEAR: I got some hankering for biscuits and syrup.

MAMA JUNE: [laughs] That damn biscuit is burnt.

HORNY BEAR: Mmmmmm . . . black crust.

MAMA JUNE: [more laughs]

HORNY BEAR: It's extra crispy, scrape it off and . . . chow down!

MAMA JUNE: [makes gagging sounds]

. . . TO BE CONTINUED . . .

ROMANTIC TIP!
Dressing up for your partner can spice things up! Get creative!

Chapter 7

BEING A BEAUTIMOUS QUEEN

Family comes first over any pageant. There's a pageant every weekend. You only have a grandbaby or a youngun's born only once, you can't ever take that back.

—Mama June

As most people know, Alana was first seen and cherished by people across the country when she appeared on the TLC series *Toddlers and Tiaras*. Although never the grand ultimate supreme, Alana was a child-pageant superstar who won "lots of big trophies," and the show gave America a behind-the-scenes look at the pageant process and what goes on there. Both Mama June's and Alana's outsize personalities riveted a nation and led to Alana's own show, *Here Comes Honey Boo Boo*.

The Inside Scoop on Pageants

Many of Alana's fans wonder, "How did she get involved with pageants in the first place?" Well, wonder no more! Here's the inside story: Mama June and Sugar Bear noticed how pretty Alana was, and many friends and neighbors would remark on how she looked just like a little china doll. So Mama June and Sugar Bear got the ideal that she might be successful in child pageants. But it didn't seem like the right time; with such a large family, they didn't have a lot of free time on their hands. After Sugar Bear's mama passed away, they decided to forget the excuses and take the plunge: "Let's do this." But they still weren't sure how to get started. So Mama June began doing research and speaking to the directors of local pageants. Mama June also researched everything she needed to do to help Alana compete—the hair, the flippers, the dresses, the coaches, etc. She invested in having Alana's pictures taken professionally by a real photographer. Alana's very first pageant was the Sweet Pea pageant at the local mall. She was four years old. While she didn't win that one, Alana had a great time and the family got a taste of the pageant life. The main thing: Alana has a ton of fun doing it and loves to compete. "Those other girls must be crazy, if they think they're gonna beat me, Honey Boo Boo child!"

Alana is certainly not the typical pageant child, and that's what America loves about her. Jessica says, "Most of the girls are like twigs, but Alana's nowhere near that. She's more of a log. Or a boulder." While it's true that Alana is a regular-shaped kid, she has one other advantage that is exceptional: she is super sassified. It's her outrageous and oversize personality that has endeared her to millions of people across the country. Even though competing is lots of fun, it's true that Alana sometimes gets sad when she doesn't win. Luckily she has the unconditional support of her family. Mama June feels strongly that you have to support your children no matter what, win or lose, and let them know that you are there for them at all times. This family bonding is just as important a part of the pageants as the dresses and the routines. As Alana says, "My family's proud of me 'cause I'm the ultimate grand supreme of my family!"

Most sources agree that the first child beauty pageant was the Little Miss America pageant that took place in 1961 at the Palisades Amusement Park in New Jersey. The pageant was organized to attract more tourists to the area, and boy oh boy, did it work.

Originally, the pageant was just for teens, but it got so popular that it was soon expanded to include younger children. These days, child beauty pageants have become a huge industry and there are more than twenty-five thousand held each year in the United States. That's a lot of pageants!

There are many different types of child beauty pageants out there, but two of the most popular (which are also often seen on *Here Comes Honey Boo Boo*) are glitz pageants and natural pageants. At a glitz pageant, contestants (and parents) are encouraged to glitz up and glam up in any way they want to. You can even glitz up your pet teacup pig. These pageants have contestants with a lot of fancy hairstyles, heavy makeup, sparkly dresses, spray tans, fake teeth, and even more. ("Spray tan is like poop in a can!" says Alana.) The contestants at glitz pageants need to have a routine prepared for each segment—Alana did her Elvis Presley rock star routine—and to look absolutely flawless throughout. As Alana's dance coach says, "Glitz pageants are very, very competitive and you have to have perfection from head to toe." The natural pageants, on the other hand, have specific rules about what the children can and cannot put on. The contes-

tants are expected to look fresh faced, with more of a natural beauty. These contestants have more everyday clothing on and almost no makeup (except for maybe some lip gloss). You can still get sassified, but it's less about your Elvis costume and more about your inner diva.

Do you have a beautimous, sassified child who might be interested in getting involved with pageants? The biggest thing to consider is the cost, as pageants can run you thousands of dollars per event. As we've seen on *Here Comes Honey Boo Boo*, Alana's a growing girl and often needs to buy a new glitz dress when the old one doesn't fit. A new dress can cost anywhere from $50 to $8,000 (not cheap by any means), and needing to buy multiple dresses can really add up and put you in the poorhouse. Factor in the costs of the hairpiece, the hair and makeup artist, the shoes, the jewelry, and the pageant coach, and you're already spending quite a bit of dough. There are also fees you need to pay to register for most competitions, depending on the size. And if you're traveling to a faraway location to attend a pageant, you'll need to think about getting hotel rooms. All of this adds up very quickly, and it's enough to make your head swim!

One thing you can do to defray some of these costs is to purchase the dress or any of your other necessities secondhand, which Mama June says a lot of pageant moms do. June uses chat rooms that are only for pageant moms and she also belongs to Facebook groups that will give you a lot of information on buying things secondhand. You can also check eBay or Craigslist to find used pageant clothes and accessories.

During season 1 of *Here Comes Honey Boo Boo,* Alana participates in three different pageants. Each one is special in its own right and Mama June is supportive of Alana no matter what the outcome. Here's a recap of how Alana prepares and competes in each pageant. You can see not only that it's a lot of work, but also that they take the judge's comments seriously and invest in more practice and training in between contests!

Beautiful Faces of GA

The Beautiful Faces of GA pageant is a "natural pageant," where they judge you for you. No makeup, no tan. There are no crowns either. This is just a practice pageant so the family can hear the judges' feedback in advance of a real pageant. Mama says, "If she wins this one, I will be very proud because they are judging on her natural beauty." Alana struts her stuff, and the pageant director introduces her by saying, "Alana enjoys pageantry, mud bogging, and being with her family." Alana does a great job, but she doesn't win any of the categories in this pageant. She is very upset and cries, but Mama June points out that Alana is always a winner in her book. The pageant director says that Alana did a very good job but needs to work a lot more on her modeling and her eye contact before the upcoming Rock Star Divas and Dolls Pageant.

Rock Star Divas and Dolls Pageant

Since Alana didn't win anything at the Beautiful Faces of GA pageant and was very upset about it, the family decides to amp things up and work really hard so Alana will win something at the next pageant. Mama June is able to secure some time at the local high school auditorium so Alana can practice her routine. "C'mon, Alana!" Mama calls. "We got a lot to learn and this is the only time we're gonna be able to use this stage!" Alana starts to practice her dance routine on the stage. This routine—taught to Alana by her new coach—is much more difficult than anything she's done in the past. At this point, she knows some of the steps, but not all of them. Alana tells her mama that

she doesn't think she can do it, but June replies, "I know you can do it. Because you're Smoochie Smooch." Mama June worries that Alana is going to be disappointed again at this next pageant, but they plow ahead with several practice sessions. A few days before the Rock Star Divas and Dolls Pageant, Mama June makes sure all of Alana's outfits are together and packed up, and also gives her a healthy dose of spray tan. When the day comes, Mama June is nervous because this is Alana's first pageant with a new coach and a new dress, but she has no reason to be concerned—Alana does amazin' in the first round. "She brought the sass like she always does," Mama says. The next round, though, is when Alana dons her Elvis outfit—and everyone knows how cool you look when you dress like Santa's helper. Alana feels over-the-top sassy in this outfit and says, "C'mon, let's go win this thing!" She pulls her new dance routine off without a hitch and delights judges and audience members alike. At the end of the day, when the crowning happens, Alana wins age-division queen for four- to six-year-olds. Mama June congratulates her and reminds her, "When you do practice, it pays off, don't it?" While Alana doesn't win the grand supreme title at the very end, everyone is extremely proud of the job she has done. On the way out, the pageant director tells her that next time she needs to pay attention to eye contact with the judges.

The Sparkle and Shine Pageant

The next pageant for Alana is the Sparkle and Shine Pageant, which is about an hour away from the family home. Since Alana had to skip a pageant due to the arrival of baby Kaitlyn, this is a special makeup pageant and Alana is very excited. She's all ready with a routine she worked out with Uncle Poodle. Before getting into the car to leave, Jessica steps in dog poop, and Mama calls her "doo doo girl." Alana says, "Pageant morning is always nuts. We was late and Jessica stepped in poop. And she smelled like a poop party!" When they get there, Mama June is a little nervous because there are some serious pageant girls there to compete. But she and Sugar Bear are also confident because Alana has been practicing really hard. She also has a new dress, a new hairpiece, and a new flipper, so Mama June thinks they can pull this off. She's hoping that Alana will pull in a bigger title this time than she has in the past.

The entire family is there to cheer Alana on, including baby Kaitlyn, who is attending her first pageant. After some trouble with the lacing, Alana gets into her pageant dress and has her hair and makeup done. She looks beautiful! Mama gives Alana a pep talk and tells her that they've worked hard all summer, and she should go out there and make her proud. She tells Alana to do the best she's ever done. Sugar Bear is very excited and says he wishes the trophies were much bigger, because he knows how hard these girls work. Finally, Alana gets out onstage and begins to strut her stuff. The whole family cheers her on, including Mama, who according to Jessica sounds just like a man. ("Work it, Smoochie!") Alana does great and doesn't miss a step. Mama notes, "Once she gets in a pageant, she becomes a different child." Next up is the "outfit of choice" segment, and Alana decides to put on her new blue bathing suit, which she says makes her feel like "a giant blueberry." She feels ready to rock this portion of the competition and says she has "chicken nugget power." Alana is going to finally perform the pageant routine she worked out with Uncle Poodle, and she doesn't disappoint. As Poodle says, Alana really brings the energy and she is "spunky and rambunctious." Even though she doesn't do Poodle's cartwheel, she does a terrific job. Sugar Bear is nervous when it comes time for the crowning, but he has a good feeling about it because he noticed the judges laughing and smiling while Alana was performing.

Alana doesn't win "queen" for her age division, which is disappointing to everyone, but she does win the People's Choice Award, which is meaningful to Mama because it means she's the audience's favorite. Because Alana has worked so hard on this pageant, her parents decide to give her a little surprise while she's onstage. It's the much-loved and missed Glitzy the pig, who finally gets to make his pageant debut when Uncle Poodle brings him up to the stage. Alana is thrilled to see her old pet, who was exiled a while back: "Glitzy, I missed you!" All in all, this was Alana's best pageant to date and one of the happiest days of the year for her.

Chapter 8

UNCLE POODLE, GLITZY, AND THE KITCHEN SINK

Miss Georgia is very pretty and I don't think she farts!

—Alana

Here Comes Honey Boo Boo is known not only for the family but also for the wild and colorful cast of characters, animals, and walk-on guests who are constantly farting, feuding, and mud boggin' on the show. Let's face it—we all need a guy in our life who will alert us to where the roadkill is. Each one of these rascals is more rednekulous than the next, and they all take part in some hilarious scenes. Some of these jokers are even edible. Uncle Poodle has become a big fan favorite, but not as much as Glitzy the pig, who squealed his way into hearts everywhere (including Alana's). And who could forget the two friends who have been with the family every day for the whole show—not Glitzy's replacement, Nugget; we're talking about the trains and the gnats. This is the multi-meal chapter, so we'll also include, well, the kitchen sink . . . meaning anything that wouldn't fit into other chapters. Team Glitzy forever!

Uncle Poodle

Uncle Poodle, a.k.a. Lee Thompson, is Sugar Bear's baby brother and a regular contributor to the redneckopedia. Uncle Poodle has a little fruit in his tank—and since Alana calls any gay man a "poodle," she decided to call her beloved Lee "Uncle Poodle" as well. As Alana explains, "Ain't nothin' wrong with bein' a little gay!" Besides his propensity for starting gross fights with food, grass, or pumpkin guts, Uncle Poodle also has hidden talents as a choreographer/dance coach. Mama June decides to let Uncle Poodle teach Alana a dance routine right before one of her pageants; maybe he can teach her a little sass! Please note—not all gay men are naturally sassy dance coaches, so use caution when approaching your own uncle. However, in this case, Uncle Poodle comes through big time and teaches her an entire routine, complete with a cartwheel. Unfortunately, his redneck nature takes over when a big grass fight erupts between Alana, Pumpkin, and Poodle. Of course, being the princess, Alana thinks she won the fight—but Poodle is pretty certain that he won. In any case, both girls are obsessed with throwing grass and mud onto Uncle Poodle's professional shirt. As Poodle says, "*Redneck* ain't the word for this damn family!" But, in the end, everything works out—after the pageant where Alana performs Poodle's routine, she comes in second place and is also crowned the People's Choice winner.

Uncle Poodle is also on hand to participate in autumn activities with the family. First he helps the girls build scarecrows for the fall. They make one that looks exactly like Mama June! Alana steals some of Mama June's clothes for the scarecrow, and they put a blond wig on it. They even put her bra and underwear on it and paint nail polish over the scarecrow's socks to make it look like it has a forklift foot! When Mama June sees it, she says, "Man, I hope this scares gnats away," and Jessica answers, "It scares me away." What's the name of this scarecrow? Junecrow, of course! Sometime later, when the family heads to Troup's Farm to pick up pumpkins, Uncle Poodle comes by to help them carve on the front porch. Everyone but Mama does a great job (her pumpkin is upside down), but the messy pumpkin guts are too much for the kids to resist. Then Uncle Poodle manages to get his head caught inside Mama June's wopsided jack-o'-lantern with the hole on the wrong side. It's "The Legend of Sleepy Hollow," wearing a professional shirt.

Glitzy the Pig

When Alana doesn't win anything at the Beautiful Faces of GA pageant, she is naturally very sad and upset. Mama June and Sugar Bear cheer her up by buying her the teacup pig that she's always wanted. A teacup pig isn't like a regular hog—a teacup piggy is only supposed to grow to weigh about thirty to sixty pounds total, and they are bred to be domesticated pets. But your ordinary porker can grow to be a thousand pounds total, and they are bred to be breakfast, lunch, and dinner. They can be strong too—a full-grown hog will break all the furniture in your house looking for truffles. It's very important to choose the right one. The baby teacup that Mama and Sugar Bear are bringing home only weighs about five or six pounds. For now, anyway.

While Sugar Bear goes to pick the pig up at the breeder's, the girls attempt to put together the pig's new bed—which is actually a kid's playpen that has been repurposed to hold the teacup piggy. (We're sure they'll wash it out before baby Kaitlyn arrives.) Unfortunately, the ladies can't assemble it and Alana says, "My pig's gonna be sleepin' on the floor because of y'all!" After forty-five minutes, they decide to leave the pieces of the bed for Sugar Bear to put together. Finally, Sugar Bear arrives with the precious oinker. He's certain the whole family is going to fall in love with their new porcine pet, even though he secretly feels like this is the weirdest pet the family has ever had: "A pig is made to be an outside animal, not inside." But Shugie is clearly the most romantic and sentimental member of the family, and he's already grown attached to the unnamed hoglet he's cradling in his arms. In a rare bit of emotion, Shugie reveals his hopes and dreams for his new family member's future: "I think the pig is going to fit in as long as we show him love. Kind of pet him and play with him and let him get used to us. I believe he'll fit in real good here."

Alana is instantly in love with the new teacup pig and decides she's going to name him Glitzy because she wants to take him along to all the glitz pageants. "We're gonna make you a pageant gay pig," Alana coos to her new friend. Although the new pig is actually a boy, Alana is going to dress him up for pageants and decides that the pig can be "a little gay." Pumpkin says, "It's not gonna be gay!" and Alana answers with the definitive smackdown: "It can if it wants to. You can't tell that pig what to do." You can't tell Honey Boo Boo what to do either.

Alana gets right to dressing the pig up and planning for Glitzy to accompany her to pageants and be used in a dance routine. Glitzy's gonna help her take her pageant routine over the top. When Alana goes for a fitting for a new dress, she asks the store's owner, Miss Lacey, if she'll also fit Glitzy for a dress. Miss Lacey agrees, but unfortunately Glitzy squeals so much during his fitting that he is banned from the store. Apparently it is challenging to make teacup pigs wear clothes, and Miss Lacey brings the hammer down: "Don't bring the pig back no more!" Miss Lacey even puts a sign up in the window that says, "No pigs allowed!" Poor Glitzy, shut out of one of Georgia's finer dressmaking establishments because of his alternative lifestyle. Also, we never find out if Glitzy got his dress, which we are sure would have been fabulous.

Unfortunately things go downhill from there. After Glitzy is denied his dress, he shame-spirals into the messy world of ooo-ing on everything. The girls put Glitzy up on the kitchen table, and he ooo's all over it. Yuck! But Glitzy hasn't hit rock bottom yet. The dang pig starts waking up at five thirty in the morning, squealing his head off because he wants to be fed. (If there's one thing Mama June doesn't appreciate, it's getting woken up at five A.M. The family normally gets up around noon! Apparently Glitzy is too much of a star to help himself to a cheese-ball breakfast.) If Mama doesn't get up to feed the pig, he will squeal nonstop until she does. Glitzy has entered uncontrollable-diva mode. Also, the family simply becomes too busy to be home every time the pig needs to eat or be given water, and the girls don't exactly help as much as they should. For these reasons and others, Mama June thinks Glitzy is not a good fit for their family and sits the family down to have a talk about it. Mama thinks it's very cute to watch Alana and Glitzy play together—Alana sometimes sleeps with Glitzy in her bed and sometimes it sounds like Glitzy is saying Alana's name when he squeals: A-LA-NA! A-LA-NA!—but it's hard to keep a pig in the house. Even a pig as fabulous as Glitzy. Mama says Glitzy would be better off in a home that has more time for him. Of course, Alana is devastated and doesn't want to give the pig up. No one asks Shugie what he thinks, but it's obvious he's just as broken up about it as Alana. Sugar Bear has a soft spot for outdoor animals that live indoors. Alana has a few last moments with the pig before Sugar Bear takes him in the pickup truck to return him. Awwwww! But all's well that ends well for Glitzy the pig. At the end of Alana's best pageant performance so far—where she comes in second place and is crowned the winner of the People's

Choice Award—the pageant's director announces that there's a big surprise for Alana. Just then, Uncle Poodle walks up the aisle with Glitzy in hand, fresh from teacup-pig rehab! Alana is extremely excited and says, "He done got bigger!"

And since leaving the show, Glitzy has been busy himself. He's been pitching his own reality television show about what it's like to be a gay teacup pig in the South, and you can find his photos on a teacup-pig social networking site called Oinker.

Are you and your family interested in owning a teacup pig like Glitzy? Teacup pigs have become very popular pets in recent years—even Paris Hilton owns one and has been photographed numerous times with it. But owning one of these intelligent animals is not as easy as it may look, as demonstrated by the Shannon/Thompson family's unsuccessful attempt! Be sure to thoroughly research what the animal is like to have as a pet, and in addition, be sure to check local laws in your state to make sure it's legal to keep one. If you do decide you want to give it an oink—um, a whirl—then below is some sound advice to get you started.

TIP #1: Pigs live a long time! Teacup pigs can live up to twenty years, so think long and hard about whether this is a commitment you can make. Think about your family and your lifestyle, and read as much as you can about teacup pigs before contacting a breeder.

TIP #2: Pigs are pretty disgusting! They scrounge for food all day long, squeal if they're hungry, poop anywhere (as demonstrated by Glitzy and the table), and generally keep their area looking, well, like a pigpen. Although many sources say you can potty train your pig, you or somebody in your family still must be committed to many years of cleaning up the pet's living space, sometimes several times in one day. Is this something you're ready for? Be honest with yourself. Maybe it would be easier to just have a human baby instead.

TIP #3: That pig ain't no teacup! While teacup pigs are much smaller than regular pigs—which can grow to weigh as much as a thousand pounds—teacups can still get very large. Often the breeder will guesstimate how big the pig will become, but the guess is not always accurate and the pig can get bigger than expected. They grow every year, and while yours might stay small, if you're unlucky the pig could reach up to two hundred fifty or three hundred pounds. That's basically the size of the world's largest dog. While a pet this size can certainly be manageable, most people who buy a teacup pig expect it to stay six or eight pounds for the rest of its adorable life. Just be aware that you can purchase a mouse and end up with a dang elephant.

TIP #4: If the love affair is over . . . Are you feeling overwhelmed? Can you just not cope with the five A.M. feedings? . . . The constant pooping? . . . We are talking about pigs, right? If your cute little porker is suddenly a two-hundred-pound behemoth that you can no longer care for, start by calling the breeder to ask if they can suggest a rescue or shelter that can take care of your previously precious pet. Or you can look online for a pig shelter or pig sanctuary or similar organization that may be able to help arrange an adoption. Don't neglect your precious porcine companion—find him a new home where he can happily live out his years without having to worry about becoming bacon, hog jowl, or trotters. When you're talking about teacup pigs, it's NOT better to have loved and lost than never to have loved at all—don't get one unless you're ready to commit!

Nugget the Chicken

After Glitzy exits the picture, Mama June starts looking around to find just the right pet for Alana. Will it be a wild ferret? A man-eating python? Or if Shugie gets his way, perhaps an adorable baby deer? None of the above! Mama June finds the perfect pet in an undersize chicken who loves to perch on her shoulder like she's a redneck pirate. Naturally, Alana names the chicken Nugget because Alana loves chicken nuggets. Nugget has an outdoor pen and actually spends most of her time outside, but Alana loves to get Nugget out of her cage and bring her in the house. This makes a mess for Mama June to clean up as the bird hops around the living room. "Nugget poops wherever she well pleases," Alana says. "And so do I." Thankfully Nugget's poop is as green as Mama June's carpet, so it all blends in at the end of the day. Nugget loves to land on all of the girls (hair, arms, everywhere) and cluck her little brains out. She's also a very strong pecker. Alana loves Nugget and Nugget loves Alana—they're a match made in pet heaven! However, the rest of the family might have somewhat mixed feelings about getting another edible pet.

ALANA: How much do you like [Nugget], Jessica?

JESSICA: Enough to eat it.

ALANA: Is it better than Glitzy, though?

JESSICA: Oh, I don't know. Both of them are good.
Because you can both eat 'em.

After a bit, Jessica admits that the chances of her trying to eat Nugget are pretty slim, since the chicken has no meat to speak of and is almost entirely feathers. "That's not even one chicken," she says. "That might be half a chicken nugget." Nugget isn't really all that small: at Christmastime, the family can't find a tree topper and decides to use Nugget instead, knocking the entire tree over in the process (don't tell Sugar Bear—it's a family secret). As with Glitzy, most of the family thinks it's just nuts to bring a chicken inside the house, but that's just the way Alana likes it.

Interested in getting your cluck on at home? Just remember that raising a chicken, like raising a teacup pig, will be a lot of work, hassle, and expense. The good news is that chickens have great personalities and will produce eggs, which will be fresher and yummier than what you can get at a grocery store. First of all, check with your town's local laws and ordinances to make sure you're allowed to raise chickens. Some towns don't allow it, and you don't want to have to return your chicken (just look at how poor Glitzy feels). Most people won't want their chickens running around the living room and pooping on their carpet, even if the poop will blend right in, so you'll need to set up a coop in the backyard. (Remember: Nugget actually spends most of her time in her outdoor coop, not on Mama June's shoulder.) The coop needs to be large enough for you to stand in and gather eggs, and it should also hold a feeder, water dispensers, and a nest for each chicken. Chicken feed can be expensive (depending on how many chickens you have) and you will need to feed and water the chickens every single day. You will also need to collect eggs every single day. Also, keep in mind that if you go on vacation, it might be difficult to find somebody to check in on your chickens and gather the eggs. If

TIP! If you're in the market for a chicken, don't buy a rooster by mistake. Especially if you like to sleep late or if you're looking forward to fresh eggs.

you're still interested in raising a chicken or two (after seeing how awesome Nugget is on *Here Comes Honey Boo Boo*), there are several books and websites, such as Backyard Chickens.com, that will tell you everything you need to know about keeping these incredible birds. Good cluck cluck cluuuuuuuck!

The Deer Statues

The most redneckulous romance on *Here Comes Honey Boo Boo* isn't between Shugie and Mama June—it's between Sugar Bear and the deer statues that now sit on the front stoop of the home. For some reason Sugar Bear can't stop talking about deer . . . or buying fifty-pound deer statues that he tries to give to June (we know they're really presents for himself). Whenever Sugar Bear is around his deer statues, he can be seen fondly petting them between their golden ears. "We got a connection with deer," Sugar explains, "because we love to get roadkill, and we like to clean it, grind it up, process it, put it in the freezer, then on the weekends get the grill out and have a good time."

Sugar Bear gets his first golden deer statue when he tries to give it to Mama June as a surprise present on their anniversary date. Shugie struggles to carry the heavy present while clutching a rose between his teeth. Although June is a bit disappointed to get the statue, she remains gracious and diplomatic: "What the hell?" she says upon unwrapping the present. "That's an unusual gift 'cause I'm not, like, into statues and stuff. Candles would have been better. I don't know." Sugar Bear is characteristically unperturbed: "I like the deer. I gotta figure out a name for him."

The second golden deer statue arrives at Christmastime. "This thing's heavy, Mama," Alana says as she pushes the wrapped present toward Mama June. "Is it a used Crock-Pot?" asks Pumpkin. "Nope. It's another golden deer statue. I got another damned deer," says Mama June. "Why do you keep buying deer, though? You know I don't like deer!" The girls say Mama never likes anything Shugie buys for her, but June says she would like it if he got her something she was into (like candles!). Soon Sugar Bear is carrying the second deer statue outside so it can stand next to the first one by the stairs. "Some people got lions to protect their house," says Sugar Bear. "I got deer."

Will there be more deer statues in the future? "He tries to be romantic," says Mama June. "But deer are not romantic to me." They sure are romantic to Sugar Bear, though. "It's no matter that June don't like deer," he says. "Just more deer for me."

Miss Georgia 2011

In order to reach her goal of becoming the ultimate grand supreme number one pageant superstar, Honey Boo Boo arranges to get some advice from someone who has already taken the crown—Miss Georgia 2011. One day, Mama June and Alana head over to the Chic Boutique to meet Miss Georgia 2011, Michaela Lackey, who Mama June arranged to meet through a friend of a friend. Alana and Mama are going to spend the day with Miss Georgia, shopping and eating lunch, and perhaps getting some good advice for Alana about competing in pageants. Alana is excited to meet Michaela and "learn all of her beauty tricks." And Michaela is hoping to give Alana lots of tips on the upcoming pageants that she will be participating in, and any advice that she needs to reach her goals. Alana and Michaela shop around, and Alana tries on everything from sunglasses to dresses while running around the store and looking in every single mirror. "I like sparkly things," says Alana. And Michaela notes that Alana definitely has enough attitude to get out onstage and not be afraid to show who she really is. After shopping for a while, the three ladies decide to go get some lunch while Alana peppers Michaela with questions. ("Are you this tall in real life?" asks Alana. "This is real life,"

Michaela replies.) Michaela tells Alana that she should listen to the judges and work on what they say to work on, such as eye contact and looking directly at the judges. After lunch, Alana's "attitude" shines through when she picks two different slices of cake for dessert and lets the cake hang right out of her mouth. "That's not cute. That's not cute. Let's not do that," suggests Miss Georgia 2011. Alana also eats cake as she's talking and actually spits food right onto Miss Georgia. Mama June reprimands her, but Alana has a very reasonable explanation: "If I don't talk with my mouth full, when am I gonna talk?" After the cake, Alana has what Miss Georgia describes as "a little incident": she farts at the table. "I farted," Alana whispers to Michaela. As we remember from our etiquette classes, farting at the table is not very etiquettely! But Miss Georgia *is* very etiquettely and politely reminds Alana that she'll need to work on her manners if she's going to keep competing.

Says Alana, "Miss Georgia is very pretty and I don't think she farts!" At the end of the meal, Michaela gives Alana an official headshot of herself and proclaims, "Alana's always going to have something extra that you'll never find in another child." Truer words have never been said. Will Alana someday be ultimate grand supreme? "It's hard to say right now if Alana will be Miss America someday. I think she has a lot of refining to do. She is only six, so she has a lot of time to grow." I guess we won't know till she finally meets Donald Trump.

Important Etiquette Lessons Learned by Alana After Meeting Miss Georgia 2011

1. No farting at the table.
2. No farting at the table.
3. Don't chew food with your mouth open or talk with food in your mouth.
4. No farting at the table.
5. No farting at the table.

The Trains

Okay, so, one question on everyone's mind is . . . What's with all the trains?! Often when one of the family members is being interviewed, all you can hear is the roar of the train that runs right alongside the family's home. It's incredibly loud and actually shakes the house. Everyone has to stop talking because you can't hear anything except for that damn train. And a lot of trains go by. "During the week it's probably ten to thirty trains," Mama June says. "About every ten to fifteen minutes." You would think the family members would get used to it, but it seems the train just gets more and more (and more) annoying every day. Anna says, "We tried to dress up as genies, and it was about as crazy as this damn train. Literally. Damn train." Then she waves to the train and says, "Hey, how y'all doing?!" Alana says, "Those trains drive me crazy . . . They drive by all the time. They wake me up. They're crazy." The sheer number of them is enough to drive anybody batty. Or maybe relax them? "It's kind of like a soothing thunderstorm," says Jessica. Anna neatly sums up the situation by saying, "I hate that train. I literally hate that train."

The Gnats

As Honey Boo Boo says: "Ahhh, get away from me, gnats! Ahhh, get away from me, gnats!" Gnats are small, annoying insects that love to buzz around your face and fly into your mouth when you're trying to talk on camera. They're on the show so much that next season they're adding them to the opening credits. Every member of the Shannon/Thompson family hates gnats—the thing they hate most is probably a toss-up between the heat, the trains, and the gnats. The family's goal is to stay in the nice air-conditioned house and keep the doors closed so that the gnats stay on the outside. "I mean, you know, if the kids leave the door open the gnats will try to come in the house . . . I mean it's just like a grove of 'em," says Mama June. "Y'all done let the ******* bugs in the house!"

But what are gnats and what do they want? And why do they want to fly up your nose? Well, those gnats could actually be one of several types of bugs: maybe blackflies, midges, sand gnats, or some other type of annoying insect that may or may not bite you. They don't want your blood—most gnats eat plants or fungus and serve a useful purpose by pollinating flowers. But no matter what they eat, they're still pests. They tend to swarm in large groups, called ghosts, around dusk. And they're attracted to lights, which might be why they're always swarming around the family when they are on camera (television camera lights are bright, y'all).

So if they don't want to eat you, why are these annoying flies all up in your business? It depends on the type; some are attracted to the gases in your breath (if there were any that were attracted to the gases in your farts, there'd be even more of them around the Honey Boo Boo house). Some are probably attracted to the warmth and moisture around your eyes and nose and mouth. And some might just be in the wrong place at the wrong time. Maybe, just maybe, when you take a deep breath that poor little gnat gets sucked into your mouth and is devoured. Gnats are probably more nutritious than cheese balls, but it's still gross.

But don't be too down on the gnats. They only live a couple of weeks to a few months, and most are destined to be food for other insects or spiders. So while they're annoying, don't worry; in a few weeks every gnat that ever bothered you will be dead. And it's their descendants you'll have to deal with. Mama June has a great tip for keeping the gnats away: stuff dryer sheets in your front pockets. It works like a charm—if you have pockets. Otherwise, you'll just have to live with the bugs.

> ALANA: I'm really excited about— [gnat flies in Alana's face] I would be
> really more excited if these gnats would leave me alone.

Redneckulous Romance, Part III

Love is in the air during Christmas as Sugar Bear steps up his attempts to get some on-camera smooches from June, who is notoriously shy. "I've never been really affectionate in front of my kids," says Mama June, "so it's not going to get him anywhere." June may not like being affectionate in front of her kids, but she sure doesn't mind embarrassing them. Listen to their conversation while setting up a fake Christmas tree:

MAMA JUNE:
[holding a fake tree branch]
Here, I gotta put this back in there.

SUGAR BEAR: There's a hole right there. All you do is slide it in.

MAMA JUNE: Well, I ain't used to finding holes.

SUGAR BEAR: Well, I am.

MAMA JUNE: I know.

JESSICA: [covers her ears and wails] UGGGHHHHHHHHH!

SUGAR BEAR: Found yours, didn't I?

JESSICA: [screams and cries]
AHHHHHHHHHHHHHHHHHHHHH! Worst Christmas ever.
Seriously.

ALANA: What happened?

JESSICA: They're talkin' about holes 'n' stuff. We're supposed to
be puttin' a tree together.

There's nothing as fun as embarrassing your kids. But the holiday romance doesn't stop there. During the toy drive, Sugar Bear dresses as a pretty smexy Santa and he even gets a special visit from a beautimous Mrs. Claus.

MAMA JUNE: Santy, I'm a little cold.

SUGAR BEAR: Come get warmed up.
Bring those hot cross buns over here.

MAMA JUNE: Heh, you're crazy.

SUGAR BEAR: I'm hoping Mrs. Claus makes it to
the North Pole tonight.

Later on, Sugar Bear switches tactics: "I got me a bunch of mistletoe, so I'm gonna lay the trap and get me a bunch of smoochies from June." Shugie hides mistletoe all over the house, stringing it up with duct tape. Even in the refrigerator! And finally, in the boudoir: "Put one there and the rest in the bedroom, I know I'll get it goin' on tonight! . . . Pucker up for Shugie!"

Does it work? Mama June walks in, sees the mistletoe, and . . . immediately makes a run for it! "Oh my God! Y'all got it everywhere in my house! Leave me alone! It's attack of the mistletoes! Oh my God, no! *Nooo!*" Sugar Bear chases her around the house and eventually gets a few minutes alone in the bathroom. As Alana says, "Mama's slippery like a little piggy covered in mud."

Was he successful? Mama June says, "I was like, 'What in the hell?' He was all like trying to make out with me. Phllugh . . . Um, Sugar Bear might have got a peck or two off, but no, Sugar Bear didn't get all the sugar that he wanted." Sugar Bear says, "I'm gonna eventually wear June down, you just wait and see. If you don't believe me, just watch." Oh, we will. At least until Honey Boo Boo gets a new little sibling.

Chapter 9

WHAT MY FAMILY MEANS TO ME

My family means "love" to me.

—Alana

Everybody's a snitch in this family.

—Pumpkin

By now you know that it's all about family for Honey Boo Boo and the Shannon/Thompson clan. Family comes first! Your family is always there for you, supporting you. And also farting on you, ratting you out during bowling contests, and regifting hot sauce to you on your birthday. They're the ones who pick you up and clean you off when the mud boggin' goes wrong, buy you a glitz pig to cheer you up after the latest pageant, and give you a pan to whack with a metal spoon when you're confined to bed rest after taking a key ring to the eyeball. They don't judge you for eating sketti. Even if you're eating it out of an empty marannaise container.

The Shannon/Thompson clan drew some pictures that represent what family means to them. Rip them out and hang them on your fridge and you'll be on your way to decorating just like Honey Boo Boo too! All you'll need are a couple of golden deer statues, some hair heads, and wall-to-wall shelves of toilet paper to complete the look. Better yet, grab some crayons and markers and draw your own picture illustrating what family means to you. Draw a picture that shows a favorite memory or family tradition—like Christmas in July, or that time you built an indoor redneck waterslide. One tip: If you do rip these pages out, be sure to buy an extra copy of this book to immortalize in your own personal library—bespoke camouflage dresses don't pay for themselves, y'all!

You may hate your family traditions, and your family might embarrass you with their sexy redneckulous romance and corny jokes, but they're still your family. You can't regift them to someone else, even if you want to. When it comes down to it, your family should always have your back, even if you're going up against Pigzilla. And at the end of the day, there's definitely nobody else you should process a two-hundred-pound roadkill pig carcass with. Seriously.

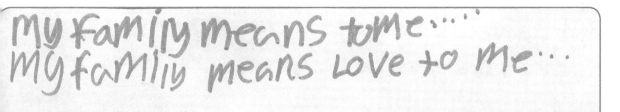

my family means to me....
my family means love to me...

Alana "Honey Boo Boo" Thompson Age: 7

My Favorite Family Memory is
Ridins 4 Wheelers

Mike SuSAr BeAr Thomes

My family means the world to me . . .

Anna Alana mama katiyln Pumpkin me

Jessica S.

My favorite family memory is...

anna (chickadee) Shannon

my favorite thing to with my family
is hanging out with our
friends and BBQ

Juno "MamaJuno" Shannon

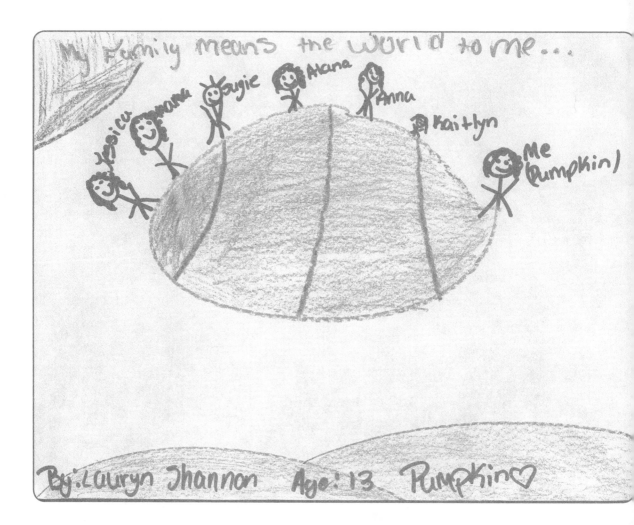

AND THEN . . .

They Got Hitched!

On a gloriously sunny day in McIntyre, Georgia, June and Sugar Bear professed their love in front of God, loved ones, and the train tracks. The color scheme of the celebration was camouflage, fluorescent orange, and pink, so June wore a camo gown with fluorescent orange trim and matching bedazzled Keds. Sugar Bear looked dashing in camo tuxedo pants, a black button-down, and a fluorescent orange vest. The girls' attire coordinated . . . mostly. Alana was the flower girl; Jessica, Pumpkin, and Anna were the bridesmaids; and sweet baby Kaitlyn was the ring bearer.

Pastor Dan, "the Redneck Preacher," officiated in a ghillie suit, at the bride's request. June and Sugar Bear got teary as they exchanged vows, and when the time came for "the kiss," June dipped Sugar Bear in a Mama-size embrace. After the lovefest, it was time to get their feast on—a whole roast pig, Southern barbecue, a snow cone truck, and a camouflage cake. With full bellies, June and Sugar Bear changed into their stretchy, casual camo ensembles and rode off into the sunset on a four-wheeler.

WHAT A BOO-TIFUL LIFE!

Bonus Chapter

HOW TO FART LIKE HONEY BOO BOO

I gotta fart.

—Anna

You've got your Honey Boo Boo name, you know the lingo, you can eat cheese balls for breakfast, and you can make your own sketti. But if you've spent any time at all watching Alana and her family, you know that the Shannon/Thompson clan has one other skill you'll need to master. And it's a stinky one.

Everybody farts!

It's true, everybody farts. Even Miss Georgia 2011. Every single person in the whole wide world farts. And Glitzy will tell you that animals fart too. Why do people fart? Why do those farts smell? Will you really lose weight when you fart? Should you be extra careful if you ever get on an elevator with Mama June? What's the most devastating wrestling move of all? Will Pumpkin really stop farting when she's dead? Read on, gentle reader, and discover all the mysteries of Honey Boo Boo's most favorite family activity. As Alana says about baby Kaitlyn, "Well, if she gets gassy she's one of the family." And soon you will be one of the family too.

So what is a fart? A fart is the way your body gets rid of some of the gases that build up inside your intestines. As the rhyme implies, if it came out the other end, it would have been a burp. Technically *to fart*, used as a verb, is to expel that gas from your buttocks. *A fart*, used as a noun, is the stinky gas that comes out. Now that we know as much about farts as any four-year-old, let's dig a little deeper into the stank. The fancy word for a fart is *flatulence*. Your friends probably call them poots, toots, raspberries, or even worse things that we probably shouldn't print. A fart is made in your stomach and intestines as a by-product of digestion. As your body tries to turn all your food into the energy your body needs, sometimes gas is made as a result. And all that smelly gas has to escape sometime—preferably during dinner, while you're posing for family photos, or in elevators.

It is indeed the types of food you eat that will determine how much you fart and how smelly those farts are, and it's going to be different for every person—though some foods make almost *everybody* fart (hello, beanie wieners!). And even animals fart—Glitzy farts on everyone. Continuously. *All the time.* And if you think people farts are bad, you haven't smelled teacup-pig farts. Why do farts smell? Mama June says, "I believe different kinds of food cause different kinds of bodily gas smells. And I gotta go take a ****." And guess what? Mama June is 100 percent right. About the bodily-gas part anyway. Eat a couple of apples. Queue one up. Now let 'er rip. Then spin around and waft the fragrance up toward your nose and take a big sniff. How does it smell? If you notice that your farts have a little extra fragrance after a satisfying bunch of apples (or a delicious marannaise sandwich), it's not your imagination. In fact, you have a superior sniffer! Science has proven that you and Mama June are correct—different foods can and will affect the aroma of your flatulence.

Can farting make you lose weight? Jessica claims, "My mother has told me in the past that if you fart twelve to fifteen times a day you can lose a lot of weight. So I think I'm gonna lose a lotta weight because I'm gonna fart a lot." Unfortunately this is an urban legend. Farting will not cause you to lose weight. Except perhaps if the fart is so disgusting that you then don't feel like eating! Needless to say, farting is perfectly healthy. As Mama June says, "If a person farts twelve to fifteen times a day then they're healthy, so I guess my girls are healthy in that respect." Farting is natural and everyone does it. But unfortunately it won't help you lose those extra pounds.

Is farting etiquettely? Farting in public is *not* etiquettely. As Sugar Bear says, "I think it's rude in public . . . but at home I don't care." If your family is okay with farting at home, let 'er rip! But you need to be able to control yourself when you're around other people. As Pumpkin found out when she had a visit from the etiquette coach, farting at the table is "the height of rudeness."

Fart Games!

Farting in front of Miss Georgia might be verboten, but when you're with your family and friends—go door nuts! Alana and Pumpkin and Jessica all use their flatulence to great comedic effect, and one game they love to play is the doorknob game. Here's how it works: If someone farts and you say "doorknob!" you can pounce on them and beat the crap out of them until they are able to touch a doorknob. If the farter in question yells "safety!" before you can say "doorknob!" then the person is safe (and the room just smells). Although this game is not unique to *Here Comes Honey Boo Boo*, the Shannon/ Thompson girls manage to make it their own. In one episode, Jessica farts loudly. Alana calls "doorknob," jumps on Jessica, and starts beating her up. Mama June asks what the heck is going on, and Anna explains that Jessica just didn't call "safety." Of course, during the family interview, Sugar Bear lets out . . . a humongous fart.

Weaponized Farting

Mama June is a fan of a tactic called the "crop duster," which is when you fart on someone and then run away before you have to smell the stink. "My favorite thing to do is kinda like crop-dust people," Mama June says. "When you're on the elevator. You fart and then you run out real quick and then the door, like, closes . . . and then they can't get out of the elevator. And you know them [people] are going to, like, the eighth floor, and you're gonna . . . Then they gotta ride up six more floors." So if you're ever on an elevator with Mama June . . . let one rip and then get off right away. Although it's not very etiquettely, the best defense is a good offense.

Another great offense is the Cup-A-Fart™, which Mama June calls "biological warfare at its best." You catch a fart in your hands and then hurl it right in the direction of the enemy's face. When Alana and family attend a wrestling match together, they encourage the wrestlers to try this move out. As Mama June says, "We're gonna revo-

lutionize the wrestling world with the Cup-A-Fart™. You just wait and see. Wrestlers will be passing out everywhere." The ultimate fart attack will cause such a stink that everyone will have to flee. This is called "clearing the room." So far only Sugar Bear has been able to clear a room, and it was a room full of professional wrestlers. That fart must have been pretty rank.

Legendary Farting

Is there really a fart ghost? "This is a spooky story about the fart ghost," says Alana. The fart ghost is a ghost that you can smell—presumably because it farted—before it scares you. Some people do think you can smell ghosts, but no one has specifically mentioned their farts. Maybe that's what dogs are barking at when they seem like they're barking at the wall. Although science has yet to prove the existence of a fart ghost, it's pretty certain that if it did exist it would be following around the Shannon/Thompson clan.

And finally, although there is probably no fart ghost, it is true that even after you die you still have one or two farts left in you as the gases in your body seek an easy escape route. Back before we knew so much about science, farting cadavers would scare people who worked in funeral homes. So although Pumpkin says that she'll stop farting when she's dead, we think she'll be relieved to know that she'll probably still have a few queued up to unleash at the right moment. A couple of stink farts are a beautimous thing to leave behind to your family. And hopefully, after you're gone, you can come back as a fart ghost and perform some crop-dustings in elevators.

AFTERWORD

*L*ast word, y'all!

In the final analysis, what is a redneck, really? Not even the Shannon/Thompson clan can agree on it. The girls say they aren't, and Sugar Bear says they are. Do you have to be missing some teeth? Do you have to like mud boggin'? Do you have to want to read this entire book? After learning how to Honey Boo Boo, we think that bein' a redneck is more a state of mind than it is a drawer full of T-shirts that don't cover your belly. It's a mind-set that says that the warmer it gets, the more sassified you become. And you can't be afraid to get muddy. It's about embracing life and all its wonderful, crazy imperfections. "We are who we are." And "It is what it is." Rednecks are all among us right now, shattering stereotypes and eating roadkill—well, that might be a little *too* redneck for some people, but you can't deny it's thrifty, and we definitely see it catching on in other parts of the country. Pretty soon they're going to be draggin' that roadkill hog carcass straight to Whole Foods so urban hipsters can fight over who gets the hog jowl. Yes, rednecks are sweeping the nation. They're a cultural force and you better damn well redneckognize—or someone's going to run a forklift over *your* foot.

But Mama June and family don't speak for all redneck families—they speak for their own. And now that you're an official unofficial member of the Honey Boo Boo family, you know what they're about: the four F's—food, family, fun, and farting. Well, and also an S: sleeping—but it was hard to work that in there. And also, saving money and charity. They are a complicated family.

Now that you know how to fart like Honey Boo Boo—and also talk like Honey Boo Boo, prepare sketti and a mayo sammich like Mama June, build a redneck waterslide like Pumpkin and Jessica, care for a teacup pig like Alana, and launch a room-clearing Cup-A-Fart™ like Sugar Bear—you've got the knowledge and the skills to redneckognize and redneck-represent. So go forth and redneckiply!

But remember, it's not the things you do that make you a beautimous queen and a Honey Boo Boo child—it's your inner philosophy. It is what it is! And besides having a blast, the whole Shannon/Thompson family put a lot of time and effort into their charity work and helping needy kids, and they believe strongly in supporting causes like anti-bullying. It's always important to give back to the community that gave you a freezer full of Logan and Darlene. It's the cycle of life. And most important, support your family and your kids, win or lose, no matter what. Family comes first, even if you have to feed 'em collard greens to teach 'em a lesson. As Mama June says, "Life is about making memories and having fun. If you're not having fun, then what's the point?" Truer, more redneckulous words have never been spoken.

ACKNOWLEDGMENTS

We don't always have a chance to give a big shout-out to everyone who has had a hand in making *Here Comes Honey Boo Boo* a success, so here's our opportunity to rednecktify that!

First of all, a huge thanks to all of our fans. We would not be here without you, and we love each and every one of you.

Thank you to the great state of Georgia and our beloved hometown. There's nowhere we'd rather be. But really, c'mon with those damn gnats.

A million thanks to our family at TLC and Authentic Entertainment. In no particular order, we'd like to thank Howard Lee, Amy Winter, Eileen O'Neill, Laurie Goldberg, Tom Carr, Rose Stark, Jennifer Pennybacker, Gail Luxton, Jennifer Williams, Meaghan Werner, Amy Savitsky, Joey Skladany, Sarah Fleming, Lauren Lexton, Tom Rogan, Sara Reddy, JB Perrette, Sean Atkins, Elizabeth Bakacs, Sue Perez-Jackson, Cady Burnes, Mindy Barsky, Bridget Stoyko, and Tracy Collins. And of course the wonderful crew—you can't imagine what they've seen. And smelled.

On the book side of things, we'd like to thank our awesome editor, May Chen, and the rest of the team at HarperCollins: Michael Morrison, Liate Stehlik, Lynn Grady, Jen Hart, Andy Dodds, Kim Chocolaad, Lorie Pagnozzi, Laura Cherkas, and Chelsey Emmelhainz. Also, a big Southern shout-out to agent Erin Niumata of Folio Literary Management and writer Jennifer Levesque for helping to bring this book to life.

And, finally, a special holla to Glitzy. You filled our hearts with squeals of love. Nugget will never replace you.